UNLEARN
THE
LIES

A Guide to Reshaping the Way We Think about Depression

Abraham O. Sculley

Unlearn the Lies

ISBN-13: 978-1-7355249-1-7

Email: info@abrahamsculley.com
Website: www.abrahamsculley.com
Instagram: www.instagram.com/abrahamsculley
Facebook: www.facebook.com/abrahamsculleyspeaks
Twitter: www.twitter.com/speaks2inspire
YouTube: Abraham Speaks2Inspire

Editing and Interior Design: Lauren Michelle
Cover Design: Thomas Anderson

This book is for the person who is hurting behind the smile, in a constant battle with their thoughts, and is wishing that someone could see beyond their mask and realize that they're really not okay.

CONTENTS

ACKNOWLEDGMENTS

I am thankful to several people who continue to believe in me and support me in all of my endeavors, especially in the pursuit of writing my first book.

Estefania Sculley, you are my rock, my biggest supporter, my best friend and the love of my life. When I am with you, I feel invincible and unstoppable. Thank you for making me feel safe to be who I truly am and for loving me unconditionally. I love you.

Othniel Sculley, thank you for being the first example that I ever had of God's unconditional, unadulterated love. You have loved me and supported me ever since I can remember. Thank you for teaching me and establishing a Godly foundation for me to build upon. I love you dad.

Karlene Donaldson, thank you for giving me life. Thank you for always encouraging me and pushing me to do better and be the best I can be. You are the epitome of hard work, dedication and perseverance and you deserve everything that you desire. Thank you for showing me what it looks like to keep fighting even through adversity. I love you so much.

Chennelle Sculley, thank you for being my second mother. You are special and you have been a powerful force for my dad and for all seven of his kids. I love you Nelly.

Thank you to my siblings, Gabrielle, Micah, Josiah, Abigail, Reuel, and Sasha-Kay for always putting up with me, challenging me to be great and making me the happiest, proudest big brother in the world. I love you guys so much.

Thank you to my great friends, Deion Pierre, Esthere Souffrant, and Joseph Jackson for always being there for me, for keeping me lifted and for always being bold enough to tell me what I need to hear and not just what I want to hear.

Thank you to all of my former teachers, mentors, coaches, and communities that I have been blessed to learn from and grow with: GRINDATION (GMEN), M.A.P.S. (Marriages and Parenting Successfully), Breathe University, Active Minds and my church family.

Thank you to all the faculty, staff and students at the University of West Florida who have helped me to grow in ways beyond what I could've ever imagined. I came to UWF as a boy and left as a man on a mission to leave my mark on this planet.

Much love, God bless!

.

UNLEARN
THE
LIES

1

DEPRESSION IS A SIGN OF WEAKNESS

"Suffering from depression does not make you weak,
it makes you human."

—Abraham Sculley

remember pacing the living room of my apartment while talking on the phone with a good friend of mine. She noticed that, for the past few weeks, I had been ignoring her calls, text messages, and I was saying no to any and every invitation that required me to leave my apartment. She knew something was up, but she didn't know exactly why I had been ducking and dodging everyone.

"Yo, what's good, my G!" I said, trying my best to manufacture an upbeat tone.

"Yo, Abe, you good?" she asked.

"Yea, of course I'm good. Watchu mean?"

"You've been ignoring my calls, I haven't seen you on campus, and you've been missing church. You sure you good?"

"Yes, I'm good. I promise."

I felt the need to defend myself. I tried to convince her that I was okay, but she knew me well enough to know that I was selling her a story, and she wasn't buying it. As I tried to find the words to explain myself, I realized that, for the first time, I, too, could no longer believe my own story. Still, I continued to tell it to see how long I could last before she found out that I was lying.

Our phone conversation lasted less than half an hour, but the pressure I felt from her interrogation made the call seem like hours. She continued to ask me question after question, and I danced around every single one, trying to make sure my story was adding up and that I was not disclosing too much information that would lead her to believe I was really struggling.

Even though we weren't face to face, she could tell I was holding back and that something was missing from my story. Then, for a brief moment that seemed like an eternity, she went silent. I could feel my heart rate increase and my breathing become shallow, and the statement that followed the awkward silence caught me way off guard. She said, "I'm not getting off of the phone until you tell me what is really going on."

I thought, *Damn, can she read my mind?*

That was the first time I had ever been challenged in that way. In the past, I had been asked "how are you?" many times, and I'd always followed with the response, "I'm good." Usually, the conversation ended there. But this time was different, and I didn't know how to respond. My friend wasn't asking out of courtesy—she was sincere, and I could hear it in her voice. I could feel that she genuinely cared about what I was going through and that she wanted to help. I also knew that she meant what she said, and if she could grab me through the phone, I would've been up against the wall with my shirt wrinkled up in her fist. She wasn't playing any more games, and she made herself clear.

I paused for a moment, and, with a nervous laugh, I responded, "Just chill…. I'm good."

She threatened to show up at my apartment and bang the door down until I let her in and spoke up. It was at that moment that I was officially terrified, and I could not let her see me like this, not when I wasn't my happy, motivated self.

My mind began to race as I tried to think of how I should respond, but I knew she wouldn't accept anything but the truth. I swallowed the knot in my throat, exhaled the little bit of air I had left, and I spoke from my heart.

That day, I confessed to my friend that something *was* wrong with me, and I didn't know what it was. I told her I wasn't able to sleep because I had these negative, racing thoughts that kept me up at night. I told her how I hadn't been eating much because I no longer had an appetite (a definite red flag in my case because I'm always eating). I told her I didn't feel like doing anything or going anywhere and I just wanted to stay in bed all day.

What happened next was completely opposite of what I had expected. Yes, she was my friend—and I knew she cared about me—but I assumed that she would either brush it off or think I was weird or making excuses. Instead, she validated how I was feeling by listening and accepting everything that I told her as truth. I wasn't aware of it at the time, but that feeling of validation was the safest I'd ever felt during that period.

After sharing all that was weighing on my heart and mind, she told me that it sounded like I was depressed. She mentioned that there were counselors on campus who were available to sit down and speak with students who were feeling the same way I had been feeling.

Deep down, I appreciated her suggestion, but I was too unfamiliar with depression in the way she spoke of it. To me, depression meant that you were weak, and I quickly shot back with, "Nah, I'm not depressed. I'm good."

I didn't accept her advice and I definitely wasn't open to seeing a counselor in that moment, but the information my friend shared with me—and the way in which she shared it—ultimately became the catalyst for how I approached my mental health and overall wellness.

It took time for me to admit the truth, but that conversation changed my perspective. It changed my life.

For the first time, I was able to see depression as an illness with identifiable symptoms rather than a sign of weakness and a character flaw. This realization and moment of acceptance was the difference between staying depressed and feeling motivated. My unwillingness to acknowledge and accept the truth resulted in a longer period of suffering, but as soon as I made the choice to accept the truth, it started me on this journey of unlearning the lies and reshaping the way I thought about depression.

Just like many people who are experiencing difficulties with their mental health, whether it's symptoms of anxiety or depression, I was reluctant to share what I was going through because I thought I was weak for feeling the way I did. At the time, I knew something was wrong, and I didn't feel like my normal self, but I wasn't fully aware of my mental and emotional condition. It never crossed my mind that I could've been suffering from depression. I thought I was just experiencing what life felt like as a hard-working college student away from home. I thought that maybe I just needed to toughen up and push through it. I now know that is far from the truth. You cannot will yourself out of clinical depression, and applying more pressure will only lead to frustration—as it did for me.

Before struggling with my own mental health, I had always taken pride in my ability to motivate others and bear the pain and discomfort of my friends and family members. It wasn't until I became depressed that I realized that I, too, could become the friend or family member who desperately needed the help and support of those closest to me. I knew how to give help, but I had no idea how to ask for or receive help. I had never allowed my family and friends to see me while I was hurting emotionally.

Sometimes when you are the "strong friend," it can give others this illusion that you are *always* strong, and it can feel out of place to be vulnerable. But even the strong friend is a human being that experiences real emotions and feelings like everyone else does.

For me, it always came easy to cut everyone else some slack, but I would find it difficult to show myself the same grace and compassion that I gave to others. My own expectation of perfection in every area of my life did not give me permission to be human. And by being human, I mean allowing myself to feel and express my emotions. I didn't allow myself to sit with my anger or sadness, and I did my best to hide my feelings of joyfulness and playfulness. I always tried to appear fearless. Many of my friends bought into the lie that I was selling of always being happy or motivated, but internally I was suffocating because I was not being true to myself. The truth is I'm not always happy and motivated. Sometimes I feel down and depressed, but I didn't know how to accept or process those emotions.

Stifling my true emotions only caused them to resurface later, like during the night when I was in bed, alone with my thoughts. Suppressing my emotions also caused them to manifest physically. I would find that I constantly had stomach pain, headaches, or tension in my shoulders and chest.

When I felt sad, I would convince myself that I had nothing to be sad about. When I felt joyful and playful, I remained cool, calm, and civilized, even though I really wanted to express my excitement outwardly.

My terrible sense of self-awareness and self-expression always came from my inherent need to put others first. I'm a recovering people-pleaser. I was so used to putting the needs and wants of others before myself that I couldn't see the value in acknowledging how I felt.

Growing up in a household where my dad was a pastor, I saw him sacrifice so much for others. My dad was known in our community as a great leader. He mentored kids in the community, he fed the homeless, he counseled people who were going through challenging situations, and he always searched for opportunities to do things for others, even at the expense of our family's wellbeing. As a child, I witnessed my dad's great need for others to love and respect him and I soaked it all in. I wanted to be just like him. There were times when my family struggled financially, but I would see my dad buy things for others who were also in need. As I got older, I adopted this same attitude of giving without expecting anything in return, even if I didn't have much to give. I wanted to make sure that I did everything in my power to get people to love and respect me.

Just like my dad, I committed to giving monetarily, giving my time, energy, love, and compassion. When I felt drained, I gave some more. You've probably heard the saying, "You can't pour from an empty cup," and it's true. We can't give what we don't have. I was so fixated on helping others that I wasn't taking care of myself. Can you relate?

One tool that's helped me to grow in the area of self-love and self-compassion has been the Bible. In the Bible, there is a story where Jesus talks about "The Greatest Commandment." In the book of Matthew 22:36-40, Jesus was asked the question: *"Which commandment is the greatest?"*

Without hesitation, Jesus responds, *"Love the Lord your God with all your heart and with all your soul and with all your mind. This is the first and greatest commandment. The second is like it, love your neighbor as yourself."* He goes on to say that these commandments are so important that we can hang all the Law and the Prophets on just the two of them.

Many Christians who read this scripture immediately hear that we ought to love God and love our neighbor, which is true, but we often miss another great lesson in Jesus's statement when he says, "Love your neighbor *as yourself.*"

Jesus is implying that we know how to love ourselves, and the same love that we give to ourselves should also be given in the relationships we have with others. The problem, however, is that many of us don't know how to love ourselves. Therefore, the *love* that we give to others is not the same love that Jesus commands us to give in this scripture.

In reading these verses alone, I learned a lesson that has transformed my life: I no longer have to feel guilty for showing myself love and compassion. As a matter of fact, showing myself compassion is the prerequisite for being able to show compassion to the ones I love. It gives me the permission to acknowledge and express my emotions, instead of ignoring and suppressing them. It allows me to be honest, open, and transparent.

If it weren't for my friend digging deep and checking on me in the way that she did, I honestly don't know where I would be today. It's scary for me to imagine what could have happened if we'd never had that conversation, but I'm glad we did.

Eventually, after a long battle with myself and my ego, I decided to seek help. I went to the counseling center on my school's campus, and, after seeing a mental health professional, I learned that there was a name for what I was experiencing. I wasn't going crazy like I thought. I learned that I was suffering from major depression.

Major depression, also known as major depressive disorder or clinical depression, is a mood disorder that causes a persistent feeling of sadness and loss of interest. It affects how you feel, think, and behave and can lead to a variety of emotional and physical problems. With depression, you may have trouble doing normal day-to-day activities, and sometimes you may feel as if life isn't worth living.

I'm forever grateful to my friend because she had the courage to create the space for me to open up, even though it may have been uncomfortable. Through her courage, I ultimately made the decision to start unlearning the lies that I'd been telling myself about depression.

What is the lie? Suffering from depression is a sign of weakness.

I told myself this lie for a very long time, and I believed it to my core. I hate being called weak, and that hate compelled me to keep my mouth shut, even during the darkest, loneliest period of my life. I thought I was weak because of what I was feeling, and it was hard for me to even consider the fact that suffering from depression may require treatment of some sort.

What is the truth? Depression is not a sign of weakness; it is an actual illness.

Here are some truths to consider if you think you may be depressed:

- Depression is a real illness, just like cancer is a real illness
- You can be diagnosed and receive treatment for depression
- Suffering from depression is a sign that your mental health needs attention
- Your feelings are valid, even if they are unfamiliar to you
- Your experience is real and you're not alone

Don't let anyone or anything guilt you into believing that you are less than because you are struggling. Believing this lie is dangerous. It will force you into isolation. It will force you to believe that you are alone, that there is something wrong with you, and that you are the one to blame and should be ashamed. However, this is far from the truth. The truth is that suffering from depression does not make you weak, it makes you human.

Unlearn the lie!

1. Admit that you have a problem. You have held on to a lie that is no longer serving you, and it will only bring you pain and shame.

2. Do your research. Go to Google and search "What is clinical depression?" Find a credible source like the National Institute of Mental Health (NIMH) and educate yourself on what depression is, what the symptoms are, and what are some of the risk factors.

3. Make a commitment to accept the truth that depression is a treatable illness.

I, _____(Insert name)_____, am now educated and no longer see depression as a sign of weakness.

2

I CAN PRAY DEPRESSION AND ANXIETY AWAY

"If a brother or sister is poorly clothed and lacking in daily food, and one of you says to them, 'Go in peace, be warmed and filled,' without giving them the things needed for the body, what good is that? So also faith by itself, if it does not have works, is dead."

—The Bible, James 2:14-17

rowing up as a pastor's kid came with a lot of pressure—or, at least, that's what it felt like for me. There was pressure to be perfect. Pressure to not say or do anything that made my family look unholy. However, along with the pressure came great benefits, one being the opportunity to develop a strong faith and trust in God, the creator of all things.

My belief and faith in God laid the foundation for who I am as an individual. One thing I learned growing up is that prayer changes situations and circumstances. My parents taught me how to pray when I was very young, and not long after, they made sure I knew all sixty-six books of the Bible and memorized a few scriptures, too.

As a family, praying was always our line of defense in any and every situation, so when it came to depression, it made sense for me to pray my way out of it. I believed that if I prayed long enough and hard enough, then it would be the antidote for treating my symptoms. I thought, *I don't need a therapist. God is my therapist.*

Prayer helped in my recovery, but I learned that I could not just pray depression away. I learned that it was okay to pray and talk to a mental health professional.

Because of my experience, I now strongly believe in mental health treatment. Prayer and therapy were a great combination. Additionally, I was blessed to have a therapist that I could pray with after many of our counseling sessions.

Another belief that I have is that you *can* be a God-fearing, spirit-filled, prayer warrior and still take medication for depression or any other mental illness. Unfortunately, there aren't many people who believe in God who are also open to mental health treatment, and they end up suffering in silence while neglecting the help being offered. I have conversations with these people often, and, truthfully, I understand their perspective because I used to share the same views. This attitude toward mental health treatment ends up being dangerous. Not only is the individual negatively affected by their choice, but they also teach their children not to seek help, and it becomes a generational cycle. The inability and unwillingness to seek help for depression, anxiety, or any other mental illness is learned, then it is passed down from generation to generation. That cycle does not end until one individual makes a conscious decision and deliberate effort to do something different and change the trajectory of their family's future. It's called leaving a legacy.

Growing up, I learned a valuable lesson from my parents with prayer being a non-negotiable in our home. Through their consistent modeling, unknowingly, my parents taught me that in order to develop a relationship with anyone, I must learn to communicate consistently and effectively. Developing a personal relationship with my Heavenly Father came from consistent communication with Him through prayer.

Naively, I also believed that prayer was the end-all be-all. Somehow, I missed the Sabbath school lesson that taught about prayer being only a part of the masterful equation. I thought if I prayed long and hard enough, then God would grant me whatever I asked for.

Additionally, due to my lack of understanding, I believed that unanswered prayers meant that something was wrong with me, that I was not spiritual enough, or that God was punishing me for the wrong I had done. Not only did I believe this to be true, but I found "proof" to strengthen my convictions. For example, in the Bible, there's a story about a guy named Jeremiah who was God's messenger. God needed to share a special message for the people of Jerusalem, and He put Jeremiah in charge of sharing the message. God told Jeremiah that He was "fed up with His own people" and that

Jeremiah should not even bother praying because He would not listen to the cries or prayers of the people anymore because of their sin against Him. *What?!*

I also found "proof" in a passage from Isaiah 1:15 that states, *"When you spread out your hands in prayer, I will hide my eyes from you; even if you offer many prayers, I will not listen."*

So, I had uncovered all the evidence I needed to justify my unanswered prayers!

For a long time, I believed that I was being punished for every wrongful act I had done in the past, and my punishment was depression. The more I tried to pray my way out of it, the more it seemed like I was sinking deeper into a black hole. My unanswered prayers made me feel spiritually bankrupt and gave me the illusion that I had been abandoned by God.

Even though this was completely false, it was my way of making sense of what I was dealing with. The truth was that God never left me, and during the moments when I felt desperation, pain, and confusion, He was right there experiencing every bit of pain with me. In Hebrews 4:15, it mentions how Jesus sympathizes with our weaknesses and the pain we feel because He was tempted just like we are. We can also trust that He will walk us through our most challenging moments because He was also vulnerable while on earth, but He overcame temptation and was without sin.

My experience with depression was not a character flaw or a punishment from God. Instead, depression was an illness that Jesus understood and was willing to comfort me through.

I was a freshman in college when I was diagnosed with major depressive disorder, and that's when I started my journey of treatment and recovery with the help of some mental health professionals. It has taken a lot of internal work for me to get to the place where I can now admit that I sought help. At the time, it was one of the biggest secrets that I kept from everyone.

There were two major reasons why I kept it a secret. The first reason was that I was afraid others would think less of me or assume I was crazy for needing help for a mental issue, an issue that you cannot physically see. The second reason was that I felt ashamed to call myself a Christian. How could I be a real Christian if I couldn't pray depression and anxiety away?

To accept help from a professional was extremely difficult because I was going against my core belief system. My belief that I was only supposed to trust in God to help me in moments of distress, especially if it was mental, something that I couldn't see. Even the idea of trusting someone to help me with a mental issue was an outward expression of my lack of faith in God. I felt ashamed. To me, reaching out for help was like saying, "God, I don't trust you to help me, so I will turn to this therapist or this psychiatrist for guidance." This belief was deeply planted in my mind, making it feel nearly impossible to uproot and modify.

Reshaping how I saw depression took countless hours of prayer, deep reflection, and a willingness to be open to new information. This willingness to proceed through uncharted territory has allowed me to see that not only does God want me to get help and be well, but He will send the best of the best to help me recover from depression or any other illness, seen and unseen.

Years ago, while playing high school football, I fractured my tibia during a game. It was painful, and I could barely walk off the field. No one had to convince me to go to the hospital, and not even for a second did I question my character because of the incident. I could clearly see that the bone was broken because my foot was practically hanging. My ability to see what was causing me pain gave me the permission to talk to a professional about what I needed to do to fix my broken bone. However, it's a different story when we experience pain that we cannot see or explain, and it becomes so much more difficult to ask for help.

Just like the pain of breaking a bone instinctively motivates us to act, the inability to get out of bed should do the same thing. Society, culture, and the media has taught us that it's normal to see a doctor for physical pain, but when it comes to mental and emotional pain, we are taught to feel shame and guilt, which prevents many of us from getting help for these issues. We negate the fact that our brain is an organ, just like our heart is an organ, and taking care of our brain health is just as important as taking care of our heart health.

The individual who has a lean body, a strong heart, and great flexibility and energy doesn't just wake up like that. It takes consistent work, and that person understands that they need to commit to a healthy lifestyle in order to maintain their physical health. Prioritizing our mental health takes consistent and intentional effort as well, and it is worth it. When we're able to think clearly, we tend to feel better and make better decisions.

Another reason why many of us run from the work required to improve our mental health is because we see it as meaningless tasks that don't bring an immediate reward. Additionally, it is uncomfortable for most people to address traumas and negative emotions from the past. So, instead, we run to our vices for quick relief. Vices keep many people suffering much longer than they need to, wasting time and money doing the things that do not fix the root of the problem. Ninety-five percent of the time, this approach leaves you feeling desperate. You can only keep it up for so long until you tire of seeing no progression or results.

I'll use myself as an example. I made the decision to see a mental health professional out of pure desperation. It wasn't until I became sick and tired of being sick and tired. Undeniably, my original approach to recovering from depression was not the most effective. There were many things that I did before sitting down with a therapist. I tried drinking depression away. I started smoking black and mild cigars. I tried distracting myself by watching porn and masturbating. When all else failed, which it always did, I went back to trying to pray depression away. I was desperate to feel better, to feel something, so I tried all that I knew to try, and I felt worse in the end.

These impulses and quick fixes never brought lasting change. In the moment, they were fantastic distractions from the internal pain that I was experiencing, and, for a few moments, I could escape. But without fail, all the symptoms came rushing back, accompanied by guilt, disgust, and shame for indulging in the things that I felt were against my values, principles, and character.

Depression was like a wound that wouldn't heal, and I was too afraid to remove the scab, disinfect the wound, and apply ointment for it to heal properly. Prior to this experience, I had never dealt with anything like depression before, and I was afraid to make it known that I needed help. Patching myself up with a bandage and hoping for the best seemed much less intimidating, but it would also leave me vulnerable to an infection—a risk that, at the time, I was willing to take.

Even today, there are still deep-rooted issues that I have suppressed throughout my lifetime and I must continue to address them, but prayer *alone* is not the answer. The Bible states in James 2:17, *"Faith without works is dead."* You can say that you have faith, but the work you do is what fortifies your faith. I learned that it was not enough for me to say that I had faith. I had to also walk the walk—and, trust me, talking is much easier than walking it out.

There is a story of a young, vibrant minister who was stranded on his rooftop after a flood had come through his city. While on his rooftop, he began to pray to God for help. After hours of praying, a couple in a rowboat passed by and yelled to the young minister, "Jump down into our boat, we can save you!" The stranded minister shouted back, "No, but thank you. I have faith that God will save me!" So, the couple in the rowboat kept on moving.

Hours later, a motorboat sped by and the man in the boat shouted, "Jump down, I can save you!" After hearing this, the stranded minister responded, "No, but thank you. I

24

have faith that God will save me." So, the man in the motorboat kept on moving.

As the sun began to set, the minister could see a helicopter coming his way. The helicopter hovered over the minister and the pilot shouted, "Grab this rope, sir. I will lift you to safety!" Again, the stranded minister yelled back, "No, but thank you. I have faith that God will save me!" With a confused look, the helicopter flew away in search of other victims. Not long after the helicopter left, the water rose above the rooftop and the young minister drowned and went to Heaven. While in Heaven, he rushed over to God and, in his frustration, he yelled, "I had faith in you, but you didn't save me, you let me drown. I don't understand why!" God calmly replied, "I sent you a rowboat, a motorboat, and a helicopter. What more did you expect?"

Just like the minister, God puts people and resources in your life to help you with the things that you may not fully understand—like depression. Many psychiatrists and therapists spend years mastering their craft and sharpening their expertise for people like you and me, who, in times of distress, can come to them and receive proper help. You may be fearful to seek professional help because of your religious beliefs or your cultural background, but that fear is one that you can overcome. Because that fear was passed down to you, it doesn't mean that you have to carry it for the rest of your life. Just like you wouldn't tell someone with diabetes to just pray about it, you also shouldn't take that approach when it comes to your mental health.

Don't let your religiosity keep you from becoming the best version of yourself. For me, prayer was essential throughout my recovery from depression. I never stopped praying and believing in God. I did not give up on prayer because I knew that God would never give up on me. However, one thing I did give up on was this idea of a magical situation that required no work on my end. God did His part in putting my friend in my life to help me recognize what I was dealing with, and I had to step up and do my part, which included seeking the help of a professional.

What is the lie? I can pray depression and anxiety away.

This could not be further from the truth, especially if your case is severe like mine was. A clinical diagnosis requires mental health treatment that is oftentimes designed and prescribed by a mental health professional. It's important to become aware of all the different resources and methods of treatment so you can find what best works for you. The keyword here is *works*. Faith and prayer alone won't suffice; you've got to get to work. Make the investment in you. You deserve it.

What is the truth? I cannot pray depression and anxiety away.

Now don't take what I am saying to mean that I don't agree that God is a miraculous God and He can do all things. What I am saying, however, is that you should be effective in your prayers. Don't pray faithless prayers. Don't try to pray your way out of putting some skin in the game. Don't use prayer as a crutch. You need to commit to a treatment plan that is designed for you and execute on the plan.

When it comes to treatment, what works for one person may not work for another person. Some people do well after taking medication. There are also some people who work well with talk therapy and need to make minor adjustments in their daily habits and routines. Then there are some people, like me, who may need a combination of medication and therapy. It's also important to understand that there will be good days and bad days during this process. Some days, I felt great! The medication was working, and my counseling sessions gave me a sense of hope. But there were also days when I felt like it was all a waste of time and my life was spiraling into a dark hole. It was challenging, but I was committed to staying the course in order to get well.

I stopped waiting for a miracle to fall into my lap and I made every effort to work for my own mental and emotional wellness. This has been one of the best lifelong decisions that

I've made. If you have been waiting for permission to take control of your mental and emotional health, here it is.

Quick tip!

Individuals who can help you with depression:

- Primary care physicians
- Mental health professionals such as therapists, counselors, social workers, and psychiatrists
- Certified peer specialists
- A trusted friend or family member

Some treatment methods for depression:

- Psychological therapies (e.g., cognitive behavioral therapy, supportive counseling, etc.)
- Antidepressant medications
- Exercise
- Sleep
- Support groups
- Relaxation training
- Meditation
- Light therapy
- Self-help books
- Supplements and vitamins

Unlearn the lie!

1. Create a list of <u>all</u> the religious/cultural beliefs that you have about mental health or mental illness. (E.g., You are possessed by demons if you have a mental illness.)

2. Create a T-Chart and list the pros and cons of holding on to these beliefs. Ask yourself: "What do I gain from holding on to this belief?" versus "What do I lose from holding on to this belief?"

3. Reflect on the lists/charts that you have created. Commit to challenging any negative beliefs that may be holding you back from seeking help and bettering your mental health.

3 I CAN RECOVER FROM DEPRESSION BY MYSELF

"Be strong enough to stand alone, smart enough to know
when you need help, and brave enough to ask for it."

—Ziad Abdelnour

There are many things I can do without help. I can tie my shoelaces, brush my teeth, drive my car, do my own laundry, and even cook, but one thing I've learned from depression is that I can't go at it by myself. Neither can you.

For as long as I can remember, I have been good at being able to keep myself motivated and disciplined in the pursuit of something that I wanted to have. If there was something that I thought needed to change, then I figured out what I needed to do, and I changed it. I didn't look for anyone's advice or validation. I used willpower and perseverance to get what I wanted. This approach to life allowed me to achieve multiple successes.

As a teenager, I learned that I had the ability to increase my efforts, which, in turn, would increase my results. I attended a charter school while in the eighth grade, and it was there where I was introduced to the idea of playing organized football. When I first started out, I sucked. I did not understand the game, I was terrible at running routes, and I was too weak to lift any weights.

I remember during one of our summer practices, we had a weightlifting circuit and each player had to do a max set of push-ups with a weighted plate on their back. I remember getting set up in the plank position and signaling to my teammate that I was ready for the weight to be placed on my back. To my surprise, as soon as the plate made contact, my elbows started to buckle, and I went down. I laid there on my chest, unable to push myself back up, too embarrassed to say, "Can somebody help me?" My teammates were standing around, trying to figure out if it was an act. Unbeknownst to them, I was stuck.

After they realized it was not an act, I heard an outburst of laughter, one that I still feel to this day. Even my coach stood there in amazement.

Trying to recover—and keep my "manhood" intact—I attempted another push-up, but this time without the weight. And still, I struggled! I became the running joke that month and the following month and the month after that. Even today, my best friend still finds every opportunity to make sure that I never forget the day when I could not do a push-up.

There were a lot of laughs that came from my epic fail, but that day also served as a catalyst for my approach to life and its challenges. After realizing that I was physically incapable of lifting my own body weight, and after being laughed at by teammates, I made up my mind to become stronger, faster, and more athletic. And that's exactly what I did. I practically lived in the gym. I became obsessed with building my body to levels that I hadn't seen before. To date, I haven't had another failed push-up experience like what I had in high school. This scenario was one out of many during my lifetime where I used pure willpower and grit to become a stronger and better individual, even during adversity.

It was also during my early teenage years that I became exposed to and obsessed with listening to motivational speakers on YouTube. I would listen to speeches before bed, as soon as I woke up, even before brushing my teeth in the morning. I listened to them before football practice and before every game. I was fascinated by the speakers' enthusiasm, and I would always feel like I was ready to take on the world after listening to an audio or watching a video.

One of my favorite motivational speakers to listen to was Eric Thomas (aka "ET, The Hip-Hop Preacher"). I studied his videos, his mannerisms, and his philosophy on life. In one of his videos, I heard him say, "If you wanna succeed as bad as you wanna breathe, then you'll be successful." I internalized that saying and believed it wholeheartedly. It made sense to me, even as a teenager, that if you want anything as badly as you want the air that you need to survive, then you will find a way to get it.

As a high school football player, my interpretation of ET's statement was to work harder in the gym, study other teams and players on film, do accessory work on the football field, and cut off all distractions that were not aligned with the goal of becoming a great football player. I became disciplined in my approach, and I achieved success. However, that same approach did not work for me as a college student struggling with depression. I couldn't just do more and feel better.

My approach had to shift. Trying to snap out of depression and motivate myself out of having dark thoughts was useless. Motivation is great, and I believe in finding ways to stay motivated, but when you are depressed and can't get out of bed, "wanting it bad enough" is a foreign concept.

Depression is a beast, and it will take you out if you allow it to. It's easy to believe the lie that you can figure it all out and get through it by yourself. Because of the stigma attached to depression—or any other mental illness—it's difficult to talk about our mental health struggles. But trust me when I say there is nothing wrong with you if you are struggling with your mental health. It means that you are a human being, going through a human experience, and it is okay to talk to someone and seek out help.

We all experience sadness. If we lose a loved one or a pet. If we fail a major exam. If we lose our job. If we break up with someone that we love. It's normal to experience sadness during any of these situations. Depression, on the other hand, can creep up on you with no identifiable cause, and it can leave you feeling drained, hopeless, and even confused. It almost feels like someone snatches your soul from your body and leaves your corpse to sit and rot.... (Yes, it's like some Mortal Kombat-type sh**.)

Oftentimes, we take the same approach that we use to deal with sadness and apply it to depression. We know what to do to uplift our mood if we're feeling sad (for me, it's going outdoors or working out), but it's a whole different ball game when it comes to depression. I liken it to trying to dress a broken bone by yourself in your own home. I would imagine you'd probably grab the compression wrap from the cabinet in your bathroom, apply the Icy Hot, and wrap that sucka up. And, honestly, that game plan might work if it is a minor sprain, but once the bone is broken, you need to take your butt to the doctor.

In the beginning stages of experiencing depression symptoms, I would muster up all the energy that I had left and would force myself to get to the gym and work out as hard as I could. I would force myself to go to different social events on campus when I just wanted to stay in bed. I tried everything I could think of, but I would come right back home depressed as if I had never left. By far, one of the worst feelings that I have ever experienced was when I felt like I had no control over what I was going through, and, honestly, that feeling is worse than the pain of breaking a bone. The lie that I told myself was that I didn't need any help, but the obvious truth was that I did. Even God, after creating mankind, said, *"It is not good for man to be alone,"* and because we are created in His image and likeness, we can trust that He knows what is best for us. God also said, *"I will make a helper suitable for him [mankind]."* God knows and loves us so much that He strategically places people in our lives who are a great fit. These people may not be the ones to tell us what we want to hear, but they will be courageous enough to tell us what we *need* to hear. Our willingness to welcome these relationships will determine our ability to grow and elevate to the next level.

I remember when I finally opened up to my friend about the confusion and pain I was experiencing, it sparked a new feeling of hope. Not only did she validate what I was experiencing, she also had a name for it and a potential solution. That validation and solution I received only came after I dropped my guard and welcomed her feedback. What she said to me was not what I wanted to hear, but what I needed to hear. And I got better, not because I figured it out by myself, but because I allowed someone to speak into the areas of my life where I was most vulnerable and needed help. The truth is, you cannot see the picture while you are inside of the frame, and I had some blind spots that only someone from the outside looking in could bring to my attention.

What is the lie? I can recover from depression by myself.

I speak for many men when I say that it's important for us to feel like we have things under control and that we can figure it out. It becomes a problem for us when we lose that sense of control, which is why I held on to the belief that I could recover from depression by myself. Don't make the same mistake I made. The longer you sit and try to "figure things out," the deeper you dig yourself into a hole. Becoming vulnerable will be a challenge for you, but it is the gateway to overcoming depression. You must let go of the lie that you can do it by yourself.

What is the truth? I need help to recover from depression.

If you could do it by yourself, you would have done it already. To recover from depression, you will need a team and a toolbox filled with different tools (strategies and resources) that work for you. Your team and toolbox may look different from mine, but we both need them. In my team, I had my psychiatrist, my therapist, my two best friends, my family, and my online mentors. In my toolbox, I had my journal, accountability partner, therapy, sleep, and exercise...just to name a few.

Quick tip!

Depression is treatable. Here is a list of things that I have found to be helpful:

- Talk to a therapist or psychiatrist
- Talk to a friend face-to-face or via video
- Make a list of what you like about yourself and practice gratitude
- Go out and spend time in nature and in the sun
- Practice mindfulness meditation
- Volunteer at an animal shelter, food pantry, or anywhere that you can help someone in need
- Get out and start moving, whether it is walking, jogging, or running
- Eat healthy foods (limit sugar, limit refined carbs, add more greens, more fruits, omega-3 fatty acids, B vitamins)
- Write down your negative thoughts and challenge them.... (I will share more about this tool later)

- Develop a habit of praying and building your spiritual awareness
- Limit social media use
- Get adequate sleep
- Do one thing that you enjoy every week
- Create a daily routine
- Find an accountability partner and ask them to check in with you weekly

When it comes to your mental wellness, you must be intentional. Decide to do whatever it takes to experience wellness and execute on that decision! Many times, we create academic goals, fitness goals, or financial goals, but how often do we set goals that will enhance how we feel, how we think, and how we act? You can change the game for yourself when you prioritize your mental health, and I've just given you a list to work from. Pick what works for you and get to it, by any means necessary. I believe you can turn things around—with help and community.

Unlearn the lie!
1. Write down this statement and repeat it to yourself: "I will ask for help, not because I'm weak, but because I want to remain strong."

2. Pick up your phone and text three people who you trust. Say, *"Hey *insert friend's name*, I'm reading this book, and I realized that it's been a while since I've told you how much I appreciate our friendship. Let's work on connecting at least once a month starting today. What do you think?"* Continue to send out this text until you have 1–3 people who agree to connect.

3. Do your research. Find a group or community (online or in-person) of people who will support you in your growth and development. Write down the date you will join that group.

I CAN'T RECOVER FROM DEPRESSION—I'M STUCK!

"Insanity is doing the same thing over and over again and expecting different results."

—Albert Einstein

"Once you are depressed, you will always be depressed." "Once you receive the clinical diagnoses of depression, you will be depressed forever." These are lies. Don't believe the lies.

Even people who are living with depression can find treatment methods and coping mechanisms that allow them to experience joy and be functional and highly productive human beings. I know this to be true, but I can also empathize with someone who feels like things will never get better.

When you're depressed, it's hard to see the light at the end of the tunnel, and no matter how hard you try, optimism seems worthless, and the idea of seeking positivity can make you feel like you are setting yourself up to be disappointed.

Honestly, while severely depressed, I came to my own conclusion that this was the person I had become. Everything I had done prior to depression was all gone—all the great moments, smiles, laughter...everything was insignificant because I was no longer that person.

The longer I chose to hold on to who I thought I was (the happy and friendly Abe), the more mental and emotional pain I would experience because I would have to wake up from that fantasy and face the reality of depression beating me down like a big bully.

It was a scary wake-up call to think that I would never go back to the "old me." I had worked so hard to become a good human being.... I paid my tithes, I didn't judge anyone (out loud), I was nice to everyone I encountered, and I even made sacrifices when I didn't have much to give. And now, everything I had worked for was being stripped away from me, and I couldn't figure out why.

I felt alone, I felt robbed, and I felt betrayed. I was mad at myself because I couldn't understand what was going on inside my mind. I was upset with my parents because they didn't understand what depression was, and I was frustrated with God because I couldn't understand the reason why He would allow this disease to take my mind captive. Like Job in the Bible, I felt like everything was being stripped away from me, and all I had left was my trust in God.

I found hope in reading blogs and watching videos of people who had recovered from depression. There was a deep desire for me to find someone who felt the same way that I was feeling. Someone I could relate to.

I would binge-watch and read everything that fell under the search results of "how to overcome depression." Every time I heard a success story, I would try to convince myself that the same success would happen for me. I studied everything that these heroes would post, and I would do everything that they said worked for them. I tried meditation, hypnosis, listening to sounds with different frequencies to activate my brain waves, journaling, and so many other hacks that they spoke about. I thought, *Well, if it worked for them, it'll definitely work for me.*

Listening and reading about all these different success stories gave me some hope to hold on to, but I had to learn very quickly that, although our symptoms may have been similar, our experiences and journeys were unique. This was a hard pill to swallow. It meant that there wasn't a specific blueprint to follow that would guarantee me the results I'd hoped to get.

Learning how to walk out my own journey was a process. I had to find out what worked for Abraham Sculley, and whatever worked, I had to continue doing it and give it time to produce a valuable return. The key here is to *give it time*, no matter if it takes two months or two years. Commitment breeds consistency, and consistency breeds results.

In my own experience, medication was effective in the initial phase of treatment, and then therapy helped even more—specifically cognitive behavioral therapy (CBT). I also had a toolbox filled with self-help strategies that worked for me, like journaling, prayer, meditation, daily walks outside, listening to positive, uplifting music, reading books, taking melatonin tablets to help get adequate sleep, improving my diet, and developing a morning routine.

I cannot stress it enough: the most important part during treatment and recovery was giving it time. I had become so accustomed to getting what I wanted when I wanted it, and it didn't make sense to me that I would do all this work for my mental health and not see any results right away. I had to be patient and take the time to learn all that I could about myself during my journey.

Just because it feels like you're stuck now and there is no hope for the future, it doesn't mean that things won't get better. Believe me when I say, they do. For someone who is severely depressed, who has not found any treatment methods that work, it may be hard to believe that truth, but it absolutely does get better. Keep trying all that there is to try. Seek out a therapist, and if you have one that isn't helpful, then find a new therapist. Do whatever you must do, but don't give up on you. The mental and emotional pain doesn't last forever. Repeat after me: "Pain is temporary! It may last for a minute, or an hour, or a day, or even a year, but eventually it will subside and something else will take its place. If I quit, however, it will last forever." —Lance Armstrong

My experience in therapy

As I briefly mentioned, cognitive behavioral therapy was and is one of the vital tools I use for my mental health. In a nutshell, CBT is a therapeutic approach that teaches you how to catch, question, and modify your thoughts before they ruin your life.

The first time I stepped into a therapist's office, I was a desperate skeptic (a term I just made up). Desperate in that I wanted so badly to feel better and was willing to try anything, but a skeptic because I was raised with the philosophical belief that "what happens in this house, stays in this house." If you are familiar with this phrase, it's probably because you're black, you were raised in a black home or environment, or you've got some black friends who have done a great job of educating you on our culture.

If you don't meet the above criteria, essentially, this phrase means that you don't tell your personal business to anyone, especially a random "professional." I understand that this belief does not solely affect the black community, but I do believe that it's especially hard for us to grow past this cultural phenomenon for many reasons, most having to do with our past and history.

My first few counseling sessions felt like I was back in elementary school and we were playing the quiet game to see who could shut up the longest. It was awkward, and I just couldn't open up. It took a while—and even a couple of different therapists—for me to finally warm up and feel comfortable enough to be vulnerable.

One tool that I received and was able to utilize in therapy came from a very famous psychiatrist, Dr. Daniel Amen, who has a strategy that he calls "Killing the ANTs."[1] (I freaking love it!) ANT stands for Automatic Negative Thoughts.

When you are depressed, at least half—if not all—of your thoughts are negative. ANTs are just what they sound like: they are automatic, and they are negative. We can't stop them from coming. They just pop into our head whenever they feel like it. Although we don't have control over whether they enter our mind, we do have control over whether we choose to believe them or not. The moment we choose to believe a thought, we give it power, and that power has the ability to change the way we feel. The moment our feelings change, our behaviors and actions follow suit.

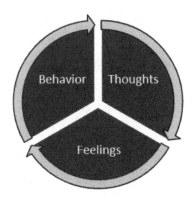

I'll use myself as an example. For a while, I had this recurring thought that I was a failure because I couldn't snap out of my depression. I believed it to be true and quickly started to feel hopeless in my situation. Once that feeling creeped in, I stopped going to classes and I'd call into work, saying that I was too sick to come in. I declined invitations to go out with friends, I ignored text messages and phone calls from people who were close to me, and these behaviors perpetuated the notion of being a failure. Let me remind you: this all started with a thought.

The thought = "I am a failure."

The feeling = hopelessness

The behavior/action = isolation

...And the cycle continues

I'm grateful that my therapist helped me to understand this concept, because depression came with a flood of negative thoughts, they all ambushed my brain at once, and I believed every last one of them.

Here's the truth: the thoughts you have are in your mind, but they are not your own. Nothing belongs to you until you grab hold of it and claim it. It's very important to understand that a thought is just a thought—they come and go.

I'll be the first to admit that I've had some crazy things enter my mind. One time, while I was driving, I imagined what would happen if I accidentally ran over an elderly person. I don't know where the thought came from, and the crazy part is there wasn't even an elderly person in sight. I've also had thoughts of walking up a staircase, only to fall and break all my front teeth. Claiming ANTs like these will only increase the likelihood of them becoming a self-fulfilling prophecy or a recurring nightmare.

Tony Robbins says, "Where your focus goes, energy flows." If you are driving, but you're focused solely on the tree ahead and you're telling yourself, "Don't hit the tree, don't hit the tree," chances are you will end up hitting the tree, even though you had to go completely off course to hit it.

What I've learned is that the more I focus on something—real or imagined—the harder my brain will work to achieve whatever it is that has my attention. My solution has been to shake myself (I literally shake my head, even slap myself, when necessary) out of any unwanted thoughts, especially thoughts of running over old ladies....

Thanks to therapy, I'm equipped with a skill to identify the ANTs, recognize how I connect to them, measure them up against reality, and restructure or eliminate them.

What is the lie? I can't recover from depression—I'm stuck.

After you have tried everything and you feel discouraged because nothing is working, I want to remind you that you haven't tried everything, and you haven't tried it long enough. During your journey, it's possible that you will feel hopeless and helpless. Depression plays tricks on your mind, and its goal is to make you think that your situation will never get better. Fight those ANTs, because once you believe that you're stuck, your brain will do everything in its power to keep you stuck.

Whatever you experience, no matter how intense it becomes, never lose hope. Hope can mean the difference between you holding on or giving up. It's that strong desire and expectation you have deep inside, reminding you that things will get better and change. Hold on a little longer and take it one day at a time.

What is the truth? You can recover from depression.

Recovering from depression will take a measure of hope, patience, and work. I am living proof that not only can you overcome depression, but you can thrive and impact others by sharing your story. I was diagnosed with clinical depression, I struggled with suicidal thoughts, I withdrew from college, and I fought for my life, but through Christ, therapy, and a whole lot of work, I was able to win the battle.

There were many times when I wanted to give up, but I kept on swinging. Without hope, you won't have the motivation or energy to make any effort to improve your situation. In fact, sometimes you will have to rely on the belief (hope) that someone else has in you, until you build that belief in yourself.

Quick tip!

Ways to build hope:

1. Write a vision statement for your health and wellness. Imagine if you were no longer depressed. What would you look like? How would you feel? Where would you go? How much energy would you have? What kinds of thoughts would you be thinking? Answer these questions in detail, and in first person, using the statement "I am..." (E.g., I am energized and full of love and compassion for myself.)

2. Reflect on a time when you experienced adversity and you overcame it. Experiencing depression may be new for you, but you probably know what adversity feels like, your ancestors know what adversity feels like, and overcoming it is in your DNA. Take time to reflect on what you have overcome in the past and allow that to stir hope within you.

3. Find someone, whether it's a family member or close friend, who believes in you so much, and listen to their belief

in you. Allow their belief in you to build your belief in yourself.

Unlearn the lie!

1. Reach out to someone who has overcome what you are struggling with and ask for their support. Ask them about their story.

2. Write down twenty-one things that bring you joy and, for the next twenty-one days, do one thing from the list each day. For example, on my list, I would write things like:

-   Go for a bike ride
-   Read a book
-   Spend time with my younger brother
-   Start a Netflix series with my wife

3. Schedule an appointment with a professional. Reach out to a mental health professional or your primary care physician and share your symptoms and how you've been feeling. You can do it!

5

SUICIDE IS THE ONLY WAY TO END DEPRESSION

"Suicide doesn't take away the pain, it gives it to someone else."

—Abraham Sculley

I knew I was in a dark place mentally when I started to become more and more curious about death. It became a slight obsession for me to overanalyze those dark thoughts. Looking back at where I once was is eye-opening because I never thought that I could've gotten so low. As much as I thought about it, I didn't attempt suicide because I was fearful of the pain that it would bring to the people I love. I also believed that if I killed myself, then I would go straight to hell. These fears kept me from acting on the suicidal thoughts, but every morning I woke up, I did not want to live, especially when living meant that I had to get up and face depression. Every day felt like torture, and I was sick of it.

Here's the thing: when you are deeply depressed, you just want a way out. You are not concerned about what it will take or how it will happen; your only desire is to wake up and no longer be depressed. Unfortunately, that desire does not become a reality just because you want it badly enough. In fact, as each day passes, it feels like you continue to fall deeper and deeper into depression.

I felt hopeless and alone and would cry myself to sleep at night, praying and yelling at the top of my lungs with my face buried in my pillow, begging God to "take depression away from me!" I would constantly ask Him "why?" and try to figure out if there was a deeper meaning and purpose behind my strife. I tried my best to make sense of it all but struggled to come up with a resolution that would satisfy me.

I desperately dug through scriptures from the Bible to console me, and I found verses like Matthew 11:28, which states, *"Come to me, all who labor and are heavy laden, and I will give you rest."* Or Isaiah 40:31, which states, *"But they who wait for the Lord shall renew their strength; they shall mount up with wings like eagles; they shall run and not be weary; they shall walk and not faint."* And then there was Jeremiah 29:11, *"For I know the plans I have for you, declares the Lord, plans to prosper you and not to harm you plans to give you a future and a hope."* These timeless scriptures gave me hope during my moments of weakness and confusion. I would speak these verses over my life with conviction, put my trust in God, and it gave me a sense of peace. However, I would be dishonest if I didn't tell you that there were also times when I struggled with my faith. Oftentimes, it was a thin line between believing wholeheartedly that God would heal me from depression and not believing at all.

I remember being home one evening, standing in front of my bathroom mirror, looking into my eyes. With tears rolling down my face and a bottle of antidepressants in my hand, I was forced to make a decision. In my heart, I knew what I wanted to do, but I was terrified to do it. I was stuck between two options. Option one was to continue taking the drugs. Option two was to stop taking them, immediately. On the one hand, I wanted to stop taking the drugs because I was afraid that I would get addicted and would need to take them for the rest of my life. Additionally, I always thought that pills were for "crazy people" and I didn't want to be labeled as "that crazy person."

On the other hand, I wanted to keep taking the medication because it helped with my symptoms, making me feel somewhat normal again. Though some days were better than others, and the medication didn't always feel like it was working, I was able to feel like myself when it did decide to kick in.

As I stared at myself in the mirror and weighed my options, I already knew what I was going to do. By that point, I had already done my research and was well aware of the potential side effects if I were to go off of the drugs cold turkey, but I felt strongly about needing to come off of the medication. As a Christian, I felt like it was wrong to depend on medication because I was supposed to depend only on God for healing. What I didn't understand at the time is that depression is not a character flaw or a morality issue; it's a brain health issue. There was a chemical imbalance in my brain, and this imbalance was not allowing my brain's neurotransmitters to fire as they normally do.

That evening, I said a prayer, asking God to protect my life, to help me to get through what was about to happen, and then I dumped the medication. That's when all hell broke loose.

After about two weeks, my body went into withdrawal. My brain would physically hurt. I felt an intense level of confusion while doing my normal daily duties. I became extremely anxious. I felt more depressed than before. My memory was trash. And I started to get these weird shocking sensations throughout my body. One of the scariest experiences would happen at random, where I would feel like I did not know who I was or where I was. I also remember being at work and forgetting my coworker's name—the same coworker I had been working with for months.

There were also many times during the day where I would overanalyze situations. One specific instance was when I texted my mom a simple message one afternoon. For whatever reason, she did not get back to me until hours later, and those hours of anticipation were devastating. My mind immediately went to: *Did I say something wrong? Did I text her at the wrong time? Is she mad at me?* After hours of overanalyzing, I concluded that she was ignoring me because she believed that I was a disgrace to our family, and, therefore, she didn't want to talk to me. Now, I had absolutely no proof that this was the reason for my mom's delayed response, but my brain made it seem believable. I had irrational thoughts regularly, and I would create justifications to confirm their validity.

Coming off my medication cold turkey brought on the worst reaction I've ever had. My brain became my enemy and it was doing everything in its power to take me out— both physically and mentally. It was as if I no longer had control.

In my mind, everything became negative, and I was the one to blame. You know how they say human beings have one side of their brain that is the "logical side?" Well, it felt like that side of my brain went on vacation and I was incapable of reasoning and making sound judgments.

I had a ton of things I worried about. I was a full-time college student who worried about not maintaining my grades. I had two jobs and I worried about not performing well and, ultimately, getting fired. I was in different leadership positions at church, I was involved in student organizations, I had counseling appointments, etc., and I felt the burden of performing perfectly in everything that I had committed to.

Loneliness also became a consistent feeling. Not only was I single, but I felt like I was alone in the pursuit of the success that I was chasing. Trying to balance everything led to me failing miserably, which was a hard pill to swallow. As a recovering perfectionist, I often need to remind myself that I'm not a bad person if I fail to meet the high expectations that I set for myself, and it's okay if I don't have full control of the outcome.

Suffering from severe depression and going through withdrawal left me feeling helpless and hopeless. The high expectations that I set for myself were impossible to reach and it no longer made sense to live if I could not accomplish what I was "supposed" to accomplish.

I became increasingly critical of myself, with no compassion for what I was going through. The more I beat myself up for not being perfect, the less motivation and energy I had to do anything else. I stopped going to classes on a regular basis, so my grades suffered, and I would consistently call and get out of work because I was too anxious to leave my apartment. During that time, I also lost a lot of weight because I no longer had an appetite like I did before.

As the days progressed, things got worse. My anxiety became crippling. I started to drink and engage in other negative coping mechanisms because I was desperate to feel better. By then, the thoughts of suicide had become even more powerful.

After repeating these cycles over and over again, I decided that it was best to pack up and go back to my parents' house. The thought of going home right after my first year, without a degree, while depressed, was the ultimate representation of failure in my book, but I didn't feel like I had much of a choice. I wasn't healthy. I was afraid of my own thoughts, and I wasn't accomplishing what I'd left home to do in the first place, which was to be the first in my family to graduate from college.

Being back home brought stability and a sense of safety, but it had its own challenges—one being that my parents didn't understand depression. Oftentimes, I found myself trying to either prove to them that I was suffering or faking it like I was all good. My parents could not grasp the fact that depression was an actual illness, that there was something going on inside my brain that made me lethargic and unmotivated. I could tell that there were times when they tried their hardest to understand what I was going through, but even their best effort felt useless. Truthfully, their ignorance to depression made it hard to be transparent, and I continued to make up different excuses for my behavior and lack of interest in doing anything.

One morning, I went for a walk like normal. I remember feeling down and I thought if I could get out and get some fresh air then I'd be able to clear my head. As I was walking over an overpass, I heard a voice in my head say, "Walk out into the traffic." As soon as I heard it, I felt a chill run through my body. I felt struck by fear and immediately started to think about all the reasons why I could not do what the voice told me to do. I thought about my mom and how she would be scarred for life if I decided to kill myself. I thought about the pain that it would bring my dad. I thought about my siblings. I thought about everyone I had ever mentored or encouraged, and I couldn't bear to transfer my pain to them. These thoughts came rushing through my mind within seconds, and I decided to turn around and rush back home.

For a long time, that experience on the overpass was a secret that I kept to myself because I was embarrassed. I felt like I was the only one who'd ever had those kinds of thoughts. I know now that I'm not. Thoughts of suicide are more common than we think, but because no one talks about it, we all feel like we're alone when we're experiencing them.

Most times, thoughts of suicide occur when we feel like we can no longer cope with an overwhelming situation, so, understanding the risk factors puts us in a position to be proactive rather than reactive when it comes to our mental health.

Here are some risk factors for suicidal ideation:

- a family history of mental health issues, substance abuse, violence, or suicide
- feelings of hopelessness
- feelings of seclusion or loneliness
- being a part of the LGBTQ community with no family support
- being in trouble with the law
- being under the influence of alcohol or drugs
- having social issues at school, or work
- having a mental illness
- having attempted suicide before
- knowing, identifying, or being associated with someone who has completed suicide
- possessing a firearm
- sleep deprivation[2]

In my mind at the time, suicide made sense. With everything that felt out of my control, the act of suicide put the control back in my hands. Yes, this type of control was destructive, but that didn't matter much. If I could end the pain and suffering that I felt, then it had to be worth it.

It's hard to realize in the moment that suicide is only a response to the internal pain and suffering, and if there is no longer any pain and suffering, then there will no longer be a desire to complete suicide. With this understanding, the goal should be to end the pain, and this can be done in other ways besides ending your life.

Although suicidal thoughts are common, it's also common for people not to act on those thoughts. There is a large gap between the number of people who think about suicide and the number of people who follow through with it. In my case, I thought about it frequently, but I never followed through because of the beliefs that I had about killing myself.

Suicide has been around for a very long time. If we look in the Bible, there are stories of men who contemplated suicide. In the book of Numbers, Chapter 11, Moses was having a difficult time leading God's chosen people, and he said to God, *"Why are you treating me this way? What did I ever do to deserve this? Did I conceive them? Was I their mother? So why dump the responsibility of this people on me? ... I can't do this by myself—it's too much, all these people. If this is how you intend to treat me, do me a favor and kill me. I've seen enough; I've had enough. Let me out of here."* In the book of Job, Chapter 3, Job had lost everything except for his life, and from his internal pain and suffering, he says, *"Why didn't I die at birth, my first breath out of the womb my last? ... I could be resting in peace right now, asleep forever, feeling no pain."* In the book of Jeremiah, Chapter 20, Jeremiah battled with depression and loneliness, and he says, *"Life's been nothing but trouble and tears, and what's coming is more of the same... Curse the day I was born! The day my mother bore me... Let that birth notice be blacked out, deleted from the records."*

It would be foolish to believe that you are the only one who has ever thought about killing yourself, and it would also be foolish to think that these thoughts and feelings will last forever. One thing that is common between each of these men from the Bible is that God was with them the entire time. He never left, not even for a moment. He didn't punish them for feeling the way they felt, and He didn't tell them to just figure it out. He sat with them in their darkness and provided a way out. In Psalm 34:18, it states, *"The LORD is close to the broken heartened and saves those who are crushed in spirit."*

One thing we know to be true is that suffering is inevitable, and there are some seasons that are tougher than others, but we can trust that God understands what we are feeling because He, too, felt pain. In Mark 14, the night before Jesus was to be crucified, He says to His disciples, *"My soul is overwhelmed with sorrow to the point of death."* Later in the chapter, it mentions that Jesus fell to the ground and prayed that, if possible, the hour might pass from him, and then He says, "*Abba, Father, everything is possible for you. Take this cup from me. Yet not what I will, but what you will.*" Jesus was clearly in pain and He probably felt every emotion that comes with suffering, so He can empathize with us while we are going through our periods of darkness.

If you are considering suicide, and you have a plan in place and a date set, I want to share something with you before you go. I have heard stories from people who were suicidal, with a plan and date in place and very valid reasons to end their life. In most cases, they had convinced themselves that suicide was the only option...the best option, but that is not the truth. Here's the truth: ending your life will end the pain that you feel—that's an absolute fact. But, while it ends the pain for you, the cycle of pain begins in the life of someone else, someone you care about, and who cares about you. Suicide doesn't take away the pain, it gives it to someone else.

Suicide cannot be the best option if it negatively effects the life of someone else. Don't lie to yourself and say that you will be helping others by killing yourself, or that your loved ones will understand the pain you were going through and will forgive you and forget that you ended your life. That's a lie. You may be right in that your loved ones *may* forgive you for taking your life, but they will never forget.

They will feel the pain, frustration, and confusion of losing you for the rest of their lives.

In the book *Suicide: The Forever Decision,* Paul G. Quinnett writes:

> *"They are angry. Though they wish not to be, they cannot but feel anger toward you. You have taken something precious from them and there is no getting it back. They are angry with you for cheating them, for rejecting them, for not giving them a chance to help you heal from what was troubling you. If they were in the wrong, then by your death you have taken away any opportunity for them to try to make things right.*
>
> *They can't apologize now. They can't learn to listen now. By your suicide, you have deprived them of any chance to understand you or to love you . And so they feel a terrible anger toward you – an anger that will fade in time, but will be there, in the back of their minds, for the rest of their lives.*
>
> *And because of this anger, they will feel guilt. They know it is wrong to be angry with you, but they will feel this anger anyway. And when they do, they will feel guilty for being angry with you. This is no passing guilt. This is guilt that will haunt them, not for just a week or a month, but for the rest of their lives. They will wonder what they did wrong, but they will also wonder why you chose to hurt them as you did. They may come to hate God as well. And they will feel guilt about this too.*
>
> *Their life will never be the same."*[3]

If you contemplate taking your own life, please know that you are not a bad person because of it. You are not evil, selfish, or crazy. You are simply overwhelmed. And there are other ways to alleviate the pain instead of ending your life.

Help is available, but you must be willing to ask for it and utilize the help once you receive it. The National Suicide Prevention Lifeline, 1-800-273-8255,[4] is confidential, and they have trained workers who are available 24 hours a day, 7 days a week to help you. But, if making the call is too intimidating, you can also send a text to the Crisis Text Line by texting HOME to 741741. These resources are completely free, and there are experts who are more than willing to listen to you and get you the help you need.

Also, don't think that you have to wait until you are in a crisis to make the call. Make the call even when you are just going through a tough time and need someone to talk to.

Even though I battled with thoughts of suicide, I did not really want to die. I just wanted to feel better. I wanted to be able to think clearly and feel like I was not alone.

Suicide is not the answer. You don't have to end your life to end the pain. You don't have to leave your family and friends. It is difficult, I completely understand, but know that you are loved, even when you don't feel like it. You matter, even when no one tells you that you do. Your life has meaning and purpose, even when you have no idea what the meaning and purpose is. You are worthy of life, and you don't deserve to die. When it feels like your situation may never change, remember that life is cyclical, your life is valuable and you are not alone.

What is the lie? Suicide is the only way to end depression.

As a child, growing up in South Florida with a loving family, I never imagined that I'd reach such a low point where I'd contemplate ending my own life. I would watch movies on TV and see different characters talking about having thoughts of suicide, but I could never relate. I thought suicide was an issue that only white people dealt with, and I never understood why they would even consider taking their own lives, but I get it now. I understand the depths of depression, loneliness, fear, and despair that can lead someone to the point of killing themselves. Suicide does not discriminate. Suicide does not care about how much money you have in the bank, where you were born, the color of your skin, or how self-motivated you are. I believe anyone can be affected by suicide, and it's important to understand this because only then will you be able to identify the signs, risk factors, and potential solutions to getting through to the other side alive.

What is the truth? Once you end the pain and the symptoms of depression subside, simultaneously, you end the thoughts of suicide.

There is a difference between wanting to end the pain and wanting to end your life. They are not the same thing. The desire to end your life only exists because of the pain you feel. The reason why suicide seems to be the only way to end depression is because it guarantees that the pain will end, but what if I told you that you can end the pain and keep your life? I would bet $100,000 that you would take that option 100 percent of the time.

I'll also go out on a limb and say that even though you may feel like you have completely lost hope, you haven't. If you are considering suicide, it's actually a sign that you are hopeful, and hope is one of the main ingredients needed to overcome depression. Einstein said, *"Energy cannot be created or destroyed, it can only be changed from one form to another."* The same is true for hope as well. Hope is not destroyed; it is only transferred. You never lost hope, it just took a different form. If you are suicidal, you may not be hopeful in the fact that your situation will improve and that you will no longer be depressed. Instead, you're hopeful that the pain and suffering will end once you kill yourself.

Although that may be true, killing yourself comes with collateral damage, and I want to give you as many tools and alternatives to keep your life AND end the pain and suffering.

Unlearn the lie!

1. You must understand depression on a deeper level! Not just as what you feel but understand it for what it is. Depression is a mental illness that has real symptoms that affect your brain and your body. If you don't understand that fact, then you will see your symptoms of depression as a sign of weakness or a flaw in your personality and character, which is false. To look at a cancer patient and say that they are weak for needing to go through chemotherapy is ignorant and unfair, wouldn't you agree? We ought to view depression the same way. Having symptoms of depression is not a sign of weakness or a result of your lack of character and integrity. Depression is a mental illness.

2. Treat the symptoms and you will cure the illness. Cure the illness and you will annihilate the suicidal thoughts. You are not depression, you have symptoms of depression, and one of the symptoms is suicidality. Make a decision to attack one symptom at a time. Don't overwhelm yourself by attempting to go after all of the symptoms at once. You are in a

dawg fight with depression, and you have to be very strategic in your attack. For example, if some of your symptoms of depression include feeling anxious, not being able to sleep well, and withdrawing from family and friends, then attack these symptoms one at a time. Let's start with feeling anxious. What makes you feel anxious? Are you anxious all the time, or is it just when you do or think about something specific? Is there a time during the day when you are not anxious? What can you do to bring down your levels of anxiety? Can you practice deep breathing or meditation? The goal is to look at the symptom and create a plan of attack so you're able to feel relief, even if it is just for a moment. Once you gain awareness from asking yourself these questions about one symptom, then do the same for another symptom. Maybe this can be done once a day, once a week, or once a month. You get to decide.

3. Celebrate your small wins! Don't get so fixated on the end result that you miss the growth and successes that you're having while you're in the game. To end depression will require patience. You must remove any timelines you have that are meant to determine when you will get well and when things will get back to normal. Control what you can and let the rest go.

Jesus says in Matthew 6:34, *"Do not worry about tomorrow, for tomorrow will worry about itself."* My greatest piece of advice is to hurry up and slow down. Trust the process, don't rush the process.

6
NO ONE REALLY UNDERSTANDS HOW I FEEL

"We're all in this together. It's okay to be honest. It's okay to ask for help. We can all relate to those things. Screw the stigma that says otherwise. Break the silence and break the cycle, for you are more than just your pain. You are not alone. And people need other people."

—Jamie Tworkowski

et me remind you that there are over 7 billion people on planet earth, over 300 million people in the United States, and about 17.3 million of those adults in the United States have had at least one major depressive episode. You are not the only one who feels the way you feel. I understand that you may feel isolated, and you probably think that no one understands your situation, but believe me, you are not that special. I really hope you don't take offense to me saying that, but it's important for me to drive that point home. There are people who have felt what you're feeling, there are people who are feeling what you're feeling, and there are people who are going to feel what you're feeling.

Understanding this reality should bring you comfort because it means you are not alone. There is someone out there who can relate to your experience. Like depression, there are many situations we experience where it feels like we are the only ones who have gone through it. The Bible says, *"What has been will be again, what has been done will be done again;*

there is nothing new under the sun" (Ecclesiastes 1:9). The things that we experience in our lives today are experiences that have already happened to generations before us.

Look at these examples and ask yourself if you've ever thought the same thing. Check the box for Yes if you can relate, or No if you cannot relate:

1. I'm in a class full of students. I don't understand what the teacher is talking about, but no one is asking any questions… I must be the only one that is lost.

    Ever felt this way? Yes ☐ No ☐

2. This is my first week as a freshman on campus and I'm nervous as hell, but every other freshman looks like they have friends and they know exactly what to do… I must be the only one.

    Ever felt this way? Yes ☐ No ☐

3. I'm about to graduate from college and I don't know what's next! I'm having occasional panic attacks, but everyone else seems to have it all figured out… I must be the only one.

    Ever felt this way? Yes ☐ No ☐

4. I do a lot of busywork to feel like I'm being productive because all of my friends seem to be doing amazing things… I must be the only one.

Ever felt this way? Yes □ No □

If you answered yes to any of these examples, then it's proof that you are not alone. This is only a list of four different examples, but, trust me, the list can go on forever!

When I struggled with severe depression, I could not even articulate what I was experiencing. Part of the reason was because I had never experienced those feelings before, and I didn't know if it was safe to share exactly how I felt. Because I hadn't heard anyone share their own experience with depression before, I was fearful of being the only one who felt how I felt. I felt drained of my energy and didn't have the mental capacity to understand *how* I felt. The best explanation I could give was that I felt "blah."

Feeling like you are the only one is a scary thing because no one wants to feel judged or ostracized from any group, even if the group consists of people you don't like. In society, it appears as though we are all well connected, but studies show otherwise. Even though we are on Facebook, YouTube, Instagram, Twitter, Snapchat, TikTok, and all other social media platforms, many people are feeling more lonely than ever before.

To avoid the feeling of loneliness, most people hang out with people that they don't even like, talk on the phone longer than they really want to, blast music through their headphones, scroll through social media timelines, or stare aimlessly at the TV. I was shocked to read a story where a lady shared that she became a mother to protect herself from feeling alone. Many people are running away from the thought of being alone, even if for just a few moments. But what if I told you that being alone wasn't all that bad? Would you entertain the idea?

My perspective on loneliness began to shift after experiencing depression, and even more so once I came out on the other side. I used to have an intense fear of being alone. I did things that went against my core values, like having sex before marriage, getting drunk and smoking weed, all so I didn't have to be alone. I was super friendly with everyone so that everyone would like me. I did everything I could possibly do to avoid loneliness. But then depression revealed to me how significant it is to be alone.

Depression forced me into isolation, and I was exposed to a side of myself that I hadn't allowed myself to sit with for too long. I began to embrace loneliness and appreciate getting to know myself, by myself. In my darkest moments, I developed a level of self-awareness that I wouldn't have been able to develop while in the midst of so many distractions. I figured out what was truly important to me. I figured out what I liked and what I disliked. I became aware of the people who were in my life for a reason, and those who were there for a season. I realized my value and significance. I also realized I was much stronger than I gave myself credit for; I not only had physical strength, but depression and isolation showed me that I had mental strength and agility. I realized that I was resilient.

All of this did not come overnight—although, at the time, I wished that it had. It took a substantial amount of time for me to understand that my experience with loneliness and depression was actually a catalyst for where God wanted to take me for the next stage of my life.

If you are depressed while reading this book, and, like me, you also believe that no one really understands how you feel or what you are going through, believe me, someone does understand.

I wish I would've known that I wasn't the only one. Everything in me believed that no one could understand what I was experiencing, and I was convinced that no one knew how to help me even if I decided to reach out, but that was the worst lie that I could've told myself.

Everyone struggles with their mental health at some point in their life. Even if it's not the same experience for everyone, we all know what pain, confusion, and loneliness feels like. Unfortunately—or fortunately, depending on how you look at it—it is a natural part of the human experience.

I saw a post made on Facebook once that asked people to share their personal experience with depression. Here are examples of real people with real experiences that so many of us can relate to:

- "I don't talk much in large groups of people, especially when I first meet them. I withdraw because of my anxiety and depression. People think I'm 'stuck up.' I'm actually scared out of my mind worrying they don't like me, or that they think I'm 'crazy' by just looking at me…" — Hanni

- "Overthinking everything and over-planning. The need to make everything perfect and everyone happy, even if it's taking all my energy. As if validation from someone else will make it all better. Sometimes I start out on high power, then just crash and don't even enjoy what I've spent weeks/months planning. And no one will see me for months after, as I retreat into my safe bubble." — Vicki

- "I smile all the time even though I don't really want to, but I do it because I don't feel like I'm allowed to be sad when I'm with other people. I also do whatever it takes to make someone else happy, because, since I don't feel happy most of the time, it just makes me feel a little better seeing someone else happy. I also isolate myself even though sometimes I really just want someone around." — Wendy

- "Neglecting to do basic things like laundry, not wanting to cook a meal or eat. They think I'm being lazy." — Rebecca

- "Going for late night walks by myself. My depression keeps me awake at night and my thoughts can get so overwhelming I feel physically crowded inside. Late night walks help me quiet the screaming in my head." — Lynnie

- "I have often been accused of having 'no sense of humor.' So wrong. Before depression took over my life, I smiled and laughed as much as the next person. Now, having lived with depression for over 15 years, the humor I find in a joke or situation is rarely visible on my face or heard in my laugh. I feel humor, but it's just too much effort to express it. I don't have the energy." — Martha

- "Purposely working on the holidays so I can avoid spending time with family. It's overwhelming to be around them and talk about the future and life, so I avoid it." — Jacob

- "Being angry, mean, or rude to people I love without realizing it in the moment. I realize my actions and words later and feel awful I had taken out my anger on people who don't deserve it." — Chris

- "Sometimes I'll forget to eat all day. I can feel my stomach growling but don't have the willpower to get up and make something to eat." — Kenzi

- "Answering slowly. It makes my brain run slower, and I can't think of the answers to the questions as quickly. Especially when someone is asking what I want to do—I don't really want anything. I isolate myself so I don't have to be forced into a situation where I have to respond because it's exhausting." — Erin

- "Saying I'm tired or don't feel good...they don't realize how much depression can affect you physically as well as emotionally." — Lauren

- "The excessive drinking. Most people assume I'm trying to be the 'life of the party' or just like drinking in general. I often get praised for it. But my issues are much deeper than that." — Teresa

- "When I reach out when I'm depressed, it's 'cause I am wanting to have someone to tell me I'm not alone. Not because I want attention." — Tina

- "Isolating myself, not living up to my potential at work due to lack of interest in anything, making self-deprecating jokes. I've said many times before, 'I laugh, so that I don't cry.' Unfortunately, it's all too true." — Kelly

- "Agreeing to social plans but canceling last minute. Using an excuse but really you just chickened out. It makes you think your friends don't actually want to see you, they just feel bad. Obligation." — Brynne

- "I struggle to get out of bed, sometimes for hours. Then, just the thought of taking a shower is exhausting. If I manage to do that, I am ready for a nap. People don't understand, but anxiety and depression is exhausting, much like an actual physical fight with a professional boxer." — Juli

If you can relate to any of these statements, you are not alone. We all feel alone until we hear someone share their story, and then it brings comfort to know that someone feels what we feel.

What is the lie? No one really understands how I feel.

The truth is that you're not alone and you don't have to go through this by yourself. Telling yourself this lie brings a sense of safety because it means that you don't have to open up and share what you're feeling with someone else. But in order to bounce back from depression, you have to be courageous. You must be willing to open up and be vulnerable because that's the only way you will overcome. Stop lying to yourself by saying no one really understands how you feel. That is fear talking. Put down fear, pick up courage, and walk in your truth. By being courageous and communicating with others, you will notice that you have more similarities than you do differences, and the people that you are closest to may actually open up about their own depressive episodes once you initiate the conversation by sharing your own story.

What is the truth? There are hundreds of thousands of people who share what you feel.

It's time to start being honest with yourself, and it's time to start being honest with others. One thing that I've learned about depression is that everyone experiences it at different levels. I view it like a spectrum: on one end you are severely depressed to the point of suicidal thoughts, while on the other side you are joyful and living life to the fullest. Each individual falls somewhere within that range. It's about becoming self-aware enough to know where you are on the spectrum, being honest enough about what you need, and being courageous enough to get help when you need it.

Also, just because we are on one side of the spectrum now, it does not mean that we will be there forever; we all go up and down as we continue to grow through life.

Unlearn the lie!

1. Take some time for self-reflection.

Answer these questions:

How do you currently feel about yourself?

_____

_____

_____

_____

_____

_____

Is there anything or anyone that inspires you? If yes, who or what?

_____

_____

_____

_____

_____

_____

Who can you depend on to be there for you when you're feeling alone?

_____

_____

_____

_____

_____

_____

What is one tough experience that you've overcome in the past?

_____

_____

_____

_____

_____
_____

What would you tell a family member or friend who is suffering from depression and may need inspiration?

_____
_____
_____
_____
_____
_____

If you had the courage to tell someone that you were depressed, who would you tell and why?

_____
_____
_____
_____
_____
_____

2. You gotta get H.O.T.

This is probably going to be one of the biggest challenges for you to accept, but I believe that you will lock in and trust the process.

H.O.T. is an acronym that stands for Honest, Open, and Transparent. Let's start with the H. You must be Honest with yourself about how you are doing—mentally, physically, and spiritually. Don't lie to yourself or neglect how you are feeling. Being honest will require you to become self-aware, which is probably not an issue for you if you are depressed, but it will also require you to put the façade down and show up for yourself.

The O stands for being Open. You must be open to change and to new information. The opposite of being open is rejecting information because it is uncomfortable or because it forces you to step outside of your own preconceived notions and learned behaviors. Being open will allow you to level up in your life because you are no longer confined by the limitations that you set for yourself. If you keep doing what you've always done, then you will keep getting the results that you've always gotten.

Finally, the T is the hardest step and the most rewarding because being Transparent is what transforms your life. Transparency means that you are being authentic. You are no longer hiding your weaknesses and keeping your secrets in the closet. Transparency breeds liberation. When you are

Transparent, it helps you to recognize that your weaknesses are what draw you closer to your Creator, and the closer you are to your Creator, the more you recognize your strength.

2 Corinthians 12 says, *"But he said to me, 'My grace is sufficient for you, for my power is made perfect in weakness.' Therefore, I will boast all the more gladly about my weaknesses, so that Christ's power may rest on me. That is why, for Christ's sake, I delight in weaknesses, and insults, and hardships, and persecutions, and difficulties. For when I am weak then I am strong."*

Being transparent is about sharing who you *really* are and how you are *really* feeling with others. I'm not saying that everyone needs to know your deepest darkest secrets, but I am saying that you need to have a trusted circle that welcomes your transparency and also engages in displaying their own level of transparency. Your environment is everything, and who you surround yourself with is who you will become. Your trusted circle may be one person or ten people, but what is most important is that you are not allowing yourself to suppress your true feelings, thoughts, and emotions.

Being H.O.T. is a process that will require WORK. It is going to be a challenge, but once you develop the habit, the reward is priceless. You have what it takes to not only accept this challenge, but to thrive in it.

Do you accept the H.O.T. challenge?

Yes □ No □

3. Make a list and make a commitment.

What are three challenges that you have been keeping to yourself?

1. _____

_____

_____

2. _____

_____

_____

3. _____

_____

_____

Pick one person from your "team" and schedule time with them to have a H.O.T. conversation.

7

ONCE I COME OUT OF DEPRESSION, I WON'T GO BACK

"Life is like riding a bicycle. To keep your balance, you must keep moving."

—Albert Einstein

I have experienced multiple seasons of depression, and they have been during different times of my life. Even though I have done A LOT of work for my mental health, I am not depression resistant. Understanding that is what helps me to commit to the work and navigate through depressive episodes whenever they show up.

I have come to realize that depression is simply a nudge—sometimes a push to the pavement—to help us become aware that something is off in our lives and that our health needs our attention. Even though I hate what depression feels like, and I wouldn't wish it on anyone, there are some benefits that I have experienced from being depressed.

If it wasn't for depression, I'm certain that I would not be as empathetic and compassionate toward others who are struggling. Before, I had a false sense of empathy. I wanted to feel what others felt in their times of distress and grief, and I acted like I understood and cared for them, but it wasn't genuine. Depression pulled emotions out of me that I didn't know I had and, honestly, didn't know that I needed to express.

I didn't know that I could be tough and cry at the same time or be heartbroken and still be a man. I was stifling my emotions and holding myself back from truly living.

There have been countless times that I can remember where I needed to release pent-up emotions from different traumatic experiences, but instead I forced myself to hold my tears in.

Depression helped me to start the journey toward healing, and a big part of healing for me was giving myself permission to cry and let go of my pain.

Nowadays, no one needs to convince me that crying doesn't take away from my manhood. My ability and willingness to be vulnerable is a sign of strength. All I need is a good romantic story, and cue the tears.

The truth about depression is that, for most people, episodes last for a duration of time. But, there are some instances where depression can be a chronic illness, with several recurrences. On average, people experience four to five different depressive episodes throughout their lifetime. It's called a relapse. A relapse is when the symptoms come back to visit after they had already left; it can be weeks after, months after, or years after a depressive episode. I don't share that to scare you, and I'm not telling you that this is going to be how your story plays out, but it's important to note that relapse is possible and highly likely for those of us who have experienced at least one episode of major depression.

Beyond the understanding of what relapse is, I also want to equip you. Most people get knocked out by situations in life because the events oftentimes come from their blind side. Depression is well known for creeping up on people unexpectedly. Don't become its victim.

As the saying goes: "Fool me once, shame on you. Fool me twice, shame on me." It would be a shame for you to have a life-altering experience and not learn any lessons from it—and trust me, there is always a lesson to be learned.

With depression, one of the lessons is being able to recognize the early signs of relapse, because it puts you in a position to make the necessary adjustments so you can prevent having to go through the same pain all over again.

Here are some early signs of depression relapse to look out for:

- You have lost interest in activities
- You are feeling unusual fatigue
- You are easily irritated or agitated

- You are having trouble falling asleep or staying asleep
- You have lost your appetite
- You have feelings of worthlessness and guilt
- You constantly feel the need to socially withdraw
- You have feelings of sadness or anxiety
- You are having trouble with your concentration or memory
- You have physical aches and pains
- You have suicidal thoughts or have attempted suicide

Here are some possible <u>triggers</u> for depression relapse:

- You have different life stressors that are overwhelming (family conflict, grief, or relationship changes)
- You are not fully committing to the treatment plan to treat the symptoms of depression
- You stop treatment too early.... Recovery is a process, don't just stop when you feel better, keep going.
- You have other health issues like diabetes, obesity, and heart disease—these can increase the risk of depression relapse

Here are some ways to prevent depression relapse:

- Commit to the treatment plan laid out by your doctor. Make a promise to yourself that you will go hard for at least six months before expecting a return on your investment.
- Check in with yourself daily. Ask yourself, "How am I really doing today?" and write down how you feel in a journal. Self-awareness is one of the most important skills you can develop.
- Help others to help you. Let family and friends know what your warning signs are so that they can check in with you when they see you showing these signs. (Visit www.notokapp.com)[5]
- Create a plan for relapse. Ask yourself, "If I were to get severely depressed next year, what would I need to do to get better? Who could I reach out to? What are the practical steps I could take to get the help that I'd need?" Those who fail to plan, plan to fail. Don't wait for the perfect time to plan, start planning now.

In Chapter 2, I talked about the lie of praying depression and anxiety away, and I made mention of the Bible verse that says, *"Faith without works is dead"* in James 2:17. In my own personal journey, the work meant that I needed to talk to a professional about what I was struggling with mentally, and I needed a specific treatment plan to overcome my challenges. When it comes to treatment and recovery, you will get out what you put in. Recovery will be a process, not a quick fix.

I didn't get that at first, but now it makes sense. I was only able to bounce back from major depression because I finally committed to the treatment and recovery process. My desire to be well far surpassed my fear of breaking the cultural barriers and unlearning the lies that I told myself. With the help of God, my psychiatrist, my therapist, family, friends, and a few online mentors, I had a plan and stuck with it. My routine had specific tasks I had to follow. I prayed and journaled every morning and every night. I always did some form of exercise every day. I had a diet plan, and I consistently showed up to my counseling appointments— whether I felt like it or not. I understood that, as a human being, I'm physical, mental, and spiritual, and I made sure that I did something to enrich my life in each of those areas. I didn't fall prey to excuses because I was on a mission. I had tunnel vision, and I believed that if I stayed consistent long enough, then I would see the results I was hoping for. No matter how long it took, I made up my mind to stay the course.

However, even though I was a man on a mission to achieve mental health, I did not plan or prepare for relapse. I worked so hard to conquer depression, and once I had beaten it, I felt like I had become invincible. I thought that once I recovered, then I no longer had to maintain it.

My routine went down the drain, I stopped going to counseling, and I threw all the positive coping mechanisms that I had learned out the door.

I failed to realize that the same thing that helped me to recover was the same thing that was going to help me stay well. I had to learn to prioritize my mental health if I wanted to put myself in the best position. Presently, I exercise five times a week, I journal, I meditate, take naps when necessary, take breaks from social media, practice gratitude, schedule therapy appointments when I experience a change in my life, I pray daily, and I do things that bring me joy.

Taking care of my mental health is my form of mental training. I believe that our mental health is just as important as our physical health, and the same level of intensity that I put into my physical training should be like what I devote to my mental training. To neglect my mental health is setting myself up for failure.

As you are working through depression, understand that you will never "arrive." What I mean by that is, you will never get to a place where it will no longer require work, discipline, and hope to maintain where you are. Sometimes the type of work, the level of discipline, or the amount of hope may change, but you will always need to continue working.

It's a privilege to be able to work, and it's our responsibility to work. Take the story of the Garden of Eden as an example. The Bible reminds us that, for six days, God went to work, creating the earth, the heavens, the trees, the sun, the moon, and all that we know to exist today. After creating humankind, the first assignment He gave to Adam and Eve was to *"be fruitful, multiply, subdue and have dominion over every living thing that moves upon the earth."* To simplify, He put them to work. God doesn't shy away from pulling his sleeves up and getting to work, and we shouldn't run from it either. Philippians 2:12–13 states, *"Continue to* **work** *out your salvation with fear and trembling, for it is God who works in you to will and to act in order to fulfill his good purpose."* All throughout the Bible there are countless examples of God expressing the importance of work. If working is that high on God's priority list, then I think we should welcome it as well.

Furthermore, God's purpose and desire for us is not to live in a suffering state throughout our entire lifetime, but the truth is that we will stay in a suffering state until we put in the necessary work to change our situation.

No one is exempt from the work required for our mental health, and no amount of money or influence will change that. There is this notion that if you can make enough money, or if you acquire enough things, then your own personal challenges will disappear.

Money and influence don't solve the problem, they exacerbate it. We hear stories of people like Kerry Washington, who stated in an interview that there was a season in her life where she struggled with her mental health and she literally continued eating until she passed out. Dwayne Johnson has been open about his personal experience with battling depression, feeling hopeless and like he was alone. Demi Lovato talks about her battle with bipolar disorder, experiencing episodes of major depression and crippling anxiety. (Check out Demi's documentary called *Simply Complicated*, where she talks openly about her bipolar diagnosis.)[6]

Along with the stories of celebrities who have struggled with different mental health challenges, there are also the irreversible cases of suicide. We have lost many celebrities by suicide. People like Robin Williams, Lee Thomas Young, Anthony Bourdain, Avicii, Kate Spade, Don Cornelius, and Kurt Cobain. Even with the success they had in their careers, they could not stand to live anymore. Success and fame can hide mental health issues for a moment, but at some point, those issues will come to the surface if they aren't dealt with.

Depression does not discriminate. Mental illness doesn't care about your socioeconomic status, your race or ethnicity, your gender, your IQ or EQ. And we all have a responsibility to take care of our mental health. I personally believe that the harder we work in school or at our jobs, the more we should engage in self-care activities to improve our mental health.

Depression is an illness that affects the brain and, if left untreated, it can lead to suicide. Depression is also a reminder that our mental health needs attention, and if we fail to do the maintenance work, even after recovering from a major depressive episode, then there is a chance we will relapse.

What is the lie? Once I come out of depression, I won't go back.

This lie comes from our own hopeful outlook toward depression and recovery. It also comes from our ignorance to how depression works. Depression is dark and lonely, and it makes sense to want to escape and never have to deal with it again. But the reality is that most people who have at least one major depressive episode end up having another episode, even after you have recovered. Understanding this fact will help you to be compassionate with yourself if you ever fall back into depression, and it will help you to become aware of your feelings so that you can identify the signs of relapse and make the adjustments that are necessary to improve your mental health.

What is the truth? If you have experienced one episode of major depression, then there is a chance that you will experience another one.

The hope, however, is that you can do something about it. You don't have to sit and watch yourself spiral. Pay attention. Learn what your specific warning signs are. Understand what triggers depression for you. Take a proactive approach instead of a reactive approach and incorporate ways that you can prevent depression relapse. You got this. Run toward the work, don't run from it!

Unlearn the lie!
1. Embrace the work. Your mental health will demand that you commit to the work for the rest of your life. Now that you are aware of how important your mental health is—it's literally the central point of how you function on a daily basis—it's time to establish a system (I call it "mental training") that works for you.

For me, mental training looks like:

a) Waking up early and having a conversation with God

b) Grabbing a hot cup of black coffee or tea in silence

c) Reciting my positive affirmations out loud

d) Doing a mindfulness or deep breathing exercise

e) Writing down 3–5 things that I am grateful for in my journal

f) Sitting down and reading my Bible

g) Completing a high intensity workout

Remember, you must figure out a system that works for you, and the only way to do that is to start now. Try different things, throw out what doesn't work, and add what does work to your arsenal.

Embrace the process of recovery. Your mental health journey is a marathon, not a sprint. There are stages that a marathon runner goes through while running, just as there are stages that you will probably go through once you decide to start your mental health journey.

Stage 1 (mile 1): Excitement

During this stage, you have unlearned the lies about depression and anxiety, you have gained the tools, you have made the commitment, and now you're ready to go! The excitement is what gives you the energy to start the journey and take the first few steps.

Stage 2 (mile 5): Denial

During this stage, you have started to implement the work. You have created a routine that works for you, you've gone to a counseling session or two, but you're not seeing any results yet. You're hopeful because it's still early in the journey, but you're also wondering if the work will pay off. Nevertheless, you don't let your doubts stop you from moving, and you make attempts to convince yourself to stick with the program.

Stage 3 (mile 11): Shock

During this stage, you are face to face with the reality that you have come this far, and it seems to only be getting harder. You're seeing glimpses of results from the work that you have been putting in, but it's not what you expected.

Stage 4 (mile 16): Isolation

During this stage, you feel like you're all alone. Even though you may have some sort of support, it doesn't feel like they are supporting the way you need to be supported. The negative thoughts start to roll in and they feel somewhat out of control.

Stage 5 (mile 19): Despair

By this time, you are convinced that you started this journey for nothing. It feels like there's no more hope to hold on to, and you're considering throwing in the towel and reverting back to negative coping strategies and going back to where you were most comfortable.

Stage 6 (mile 22): "The Wall"

During this stage, you have officially quit. You're angry because you put in all the work and still did not get the return you were hoping for. You're tired.

Stage 7 (mile 23): Affirmation

During this stage, you get a surge of energy, confidence, and perseverance—a second wind. You remind yourself that you didn't come this far to only come this far. You are determined to get a return on your investment, and you're willing to go through the hurt, pain, and doubt to overcome depression. You start to find stories that inspire you, you start talking to yourself to stay motivated, and you develop a "by any means necessary" attitude to keep moving forward.

Stage 8 (mile 26): Elation

During this stage, you have finally broken through the wall. All the work you had been putting in has finally paid off, and you feel a sense of relief and joy. Because you played an active role in your recovery, you then realize that you are stronger than you thought you were. You realize that Philippians 4:13 is not just a catchy verse in the Bible, and you genuinely believe: "*I can do all things through Christ who strengthens me.*" After breaking through the barriers that kept you stuck for so long, you now feel a sense of responsibility to share what you've learned, share your story, and help others to accomplish what you managed to accomplish.

2. Enjoy the lifelong covenant. The Bible talks about our bodies as a temple where the Holy Spirit lives. Your brain is an organ in your body, and sometimes we get so focused on maintaining other parts of our body that we forget to monitor our mental state. It's important to be mindful of what we allow to enter into our minds and what conversations we are having with others and with ourselves. Philippians 4:8 says, *"Finally, brothers, whatever is true, whatever is honorable, whatever is just, whatever is pure, whatever is lovely, whatever is commendable, if there is any excellence, if there is anything worthy of praise, think about these things."* The Bible also reminds us of our obligation to our minds and the transformation that God wants us to have in Romans 12:1-2: *"Present your bodies as a living sacrifice, holy and acceptable to God, which is your spiritual worship. Do not be conformed to this world, but be transformed by the renewal of your mind, that by testing you may discern what is the will of God, what is good and acceptable and perfect."*

To experience transformation, you must renew your mind, and that requires work. There will be ups and downs without a doubt, but don't let the ebbs and flows keep you from enjoying the journey. The road to unlearning the lies and reshaping the way you think about depression is a long one, and it is up to you to stay the course and reap those benefits along the way. I believe that you already have everything inside of you to unlearn the lies and reshape the way you think about depression. My hope is that you use this guide to aid you on your journey. Let the journey begin.

MENTAL HEALTH CHECK-IN

(Check all that apply)[7]

For the past two weeks:

Have you been having trouble with concentration?
Yes □ No □

Have you been indecisive about making decisions?
Yes □ No □

Have you been forgetting little things, like whether you locked the apartment door, or what time your class, or work starts?
Yes □ No □

Have you been feeling hopeless, worthless, or guilty?
Yes □ No □

Have you been having trouble with sleep (i.e., sleeping too much or waking up during the middle of the night)?
Yes □ No □

Have you lost interest in things that you used to love doing?

Yes ☐ No ☐

Have you been overeating or not eating as much as you should?

Yes ☐ No ☐

Do you have aches, pains, headaches, or cramps that just won't go away?

Yes ☐ No ☐

Have you been feeling "empty," persistently sad, or anxious?

Yes ☐ No ☐

Have you been having suicidal thoughts?

Yes ☐ No ☐

*If you answered "Yes" to five or more of these questions, I recommend that you see your doctor or a mental health professional and share this information with them.

MENTAL HEALTH RESOURCE GUIDE

Mobile Apps:
- Headspace—a guided meditation, mindfulness, and sleep application.
- Calm—#1 app for sleep and meditation.
- 7 Cups—FREE anonymous emotional support and counseling from trained active listeners.
- notOK™—a digital panic button that takes the guesswork out of asking for help when you're feeling vulnerable.
- Sanvello: Anxiety & Depression—#1 app for stress, anxiety, and depression.
- Abide Bible & Sleep Meditation—#1 Christian meditation app to sleep better and stress less.

Social Media Accounts to Follow:
@speaks2inspire
@abrahamsculley
@active_minds
@jedfoundation
@blackmenheal
@jckfoundation
@therapyislight
@afspnational
@crisistextline

@nimhgov
@mentalhealthcoalition
@howareyoureally
@neda
@trevorproject
@therapyforblackgirls
@blhensonfoundation
@800273talk
@namicommunicate
@twloha
@realdepressionproject
@therapyforlatinx
@mentalhealthamerica
@silencetheshame
@blackmentalwellness

Supplements for Depression:
Rhodiola
Ashwagandha
Ginkgo Biloba
Omega-3
5-HTP
Vitamin D
Vitamin B

*Speak with your doctor before trying any of these supplements.

Online Communities:
National Alliance on Mental Illness (NAMI)—www.nami.org/findsupport
American Foundation for Suicide Prevention (AFSP) —www.afsp.org/find-a-local-chapter
Active Minds—www.activeminds.org
GRINDATION—www.grindation.com
GMEN—www.gmenworldwide.com
GWOMEN—www.grindation.com
Breathe University—www.etinspires.com/breathe
The Jed Foundation—www.jedfoundation.org
The Trevor Project—www.thetrevorproject.org
Silence the Shame—www.silencetheshame.com
National Eating Disorders Association—www.nationaleatingdisorders.org
National Institute of Mental Health—www.nimh.nih.gov

Find a Therapist:
Psychology Today—www.psychologytoday.com
Open Path Collective—www.openpathcollective.org
Better Help—www.betterhelp.com

Crisis:
Suicide Prevention Hotline: 1-800-273-8255
Crisis Text Line: Text HOME to 741741

Resources for BIPOC:

Black Emotional and Mental Health Collective (BEAM)—www.beam.community/bvtn

Inclusive Therapists—www.inclusivetherapists.com

Therapy for Black Girls—www.therapyforblackgirls.com

Therapy for Black Men—www.therapyforblackmen.org

The Steve Fund—www.stevefund.org

The Boris Lawrence Henson Foundation—borislhensonfoundation.org

Facebook Group: Free Therapist Led Support Group For Those Affected By Racial Trauma

Black Therapists Rock—www.blacktherapistsrock.com

Black Mental Matters Podcast

Books to Read:

The Bible

Man's Search for Meaning by Viktor Frankl

Change Your Brain Change Your Life by Daniel G. Amen

End of Mental Illness by Daniel G. Amen

You Are a Badass by Jen Sincero

Feeling Good: The New Mood Therapy by David D. Burns

The Power of Now by Eckhart Tolle

The Unapologetic Guide to Black Mental Health by Rheeda Walker

Don't Sweat the Small Stuff and It's All Small Stuff by Richard Carlson

The Dream Giver by Bruce Wilkinson

The Book of Joy by Dalai Lama

I'm ready to talk to a therapist. Where do I start?

1. Identify what exactly you would like to work on in therapy. It's okay if you are unsure.
2. Identify what your goal is with therapy.
3. What is your budget, if any? If not, are there community resources available?
4. What insurance do you have? What is the cost to use a therapist that is in-network versus out-of-network?
5. Are you comfortable with tele-therapy?
6. Is it important for your therapist to be a specific gender, race, or sexual orientation?
7. What style of therapy do you prefer? Do you want someone to provide theory and explain things to you? Do you want someone who will take a holistic approach? Do you want someone who will challenge you? Would you prefer group therapy?
8. Find a directory and search for therapists that meet your criteria and make a list of at least ten therapists.
9. Call the offices of at least five therapist and ask if they offer complimentary consultations over the phone. If yes, let them know of your interest in therapy and share your goal(s). If cost is an issue, then ask about low-cost options (sliding scale). Use the consultation as an opportunity to ask as many questions as you can to gauge if this person may be a good fit.

10. Schedule an appointment and approach your therapy session with an open mind.

Remember, if you find that your therapist is not a great fit, it is completely fine to end the professional relationship and search for a new therapist.

Steps for Killing the ANTs[8]:
Different Types of ANTs

Always ANTs—You think in words like "always," "never," "no one," "everyone," "every time," "everything."

Focusing on the negative ANTs—You only see the bad in a situation.

Fortune telling ANTs—You predict the worst possible outcome to a situation.

Mind reading ANTs—You believe that you know what another person is thinking and it's not good. Even though they haven't told you and you didn't even ask.

Thinking with your feelings ANTs—You believe negative feelings without ever questioning them.

Guilt ANTs—You think in words like "should," "must," "ought to" or "have to."

Labeling ANTs—You attach a negative label to yourself or to someone else.

Personalization ANTs—You take an innocent event and create a personal, negative meaning from it.

Blaming ANTs—You blame someone else for your own problems.

Step 1: Bring your awareness to the ANT (write in down in a journal or in your phone)

Step 2: Challenge the ANT (Is it true? What are the facts to prove that it is true?)

Step 3: Replace it with a positive thought (write it down in a journal or in your phone)

For example:

Step 1: ANT— "I will be fired from my job because I am always late."

Step 2: Yes, I am running late, but this is the second time that I am late out of over two years of working with perfect attendance. I am not always late.

Step 3: I will apologize to my supervisor for being late and I will have an amazing day at work.

*Don't let ANTs take your mind captive. Become aware of them, challenge them, and replace them with positive thoughts. Make this practice a habit and they will no longer have power.

Vision Statement of Health and Wellness:

I am joyful. I am peaceful. I am confident about my actions and the decisions that I make to enhance my life and the lives of others. I sleep well and peacefully at night and wake up fully energized. I have great and open relationships with my family, friends, and coworkers. I look forward to and eagerly accept new challenges that are ahead of me. I am a good influence to those that I am around. I love and appreciate my body and I exercise daily. I use my past experiences to uplift and strengthen others through their difficult times. I am grateful for my life and I love and live for my Heavenly Father.

*Use this vision statement as a template to help you to create your own, or feel free to use this one

10 Inspirational Sayings and Scriptures:
1. "The Lord himself goes before you and will be with you; he will never leave you nor forsake you. Do not be afraid; do not be discouraged" (Deuteronomy 31:8).
2. "Sometimes God closes doors because it's time to move forward. He knows you won't move unless your circumstances force you. Trust the transition. God's got you." —Anonymous
3. "Hope is important because it can make the present moment less difficult to bear. If we believe that tomorrow will be better, we can bear a hardship today." —Thich Nhat Hanh
4. "Come to me, all who labor and are heavy laden, and I will give you rest" (Matthew 11:28).
5. "The Lord is near to the brokenhearted and saves the crushed in spirit" (Psalm 34:18).
6. "Hope is the thing with feathers that perches in the soul and sings the tune without the words and never stops at all." —Emily Dickinson

7. "If you can't fly then run, if you can't run then walk, if you can't walk then crawl, but whatever you do you have to keep moving forward." —Martin Luther King Jr.

8. "For I am convinced that neither death nor life, neither angels nor demons, neither the present nor the future, nor any powers, neither height nor depth, nor anything else in all creation, will be able to separate us from the love of God that is in Christ Jesus our Lord" (Romans 8:38-39).

9. "Learn from yesterday, live for today, hope for tomorrow. The important thing is not to stop questioning." —Albert Einstein

10. "And we know that all things work together for good to them that love God, to them who are the called according to His purpose" (Romans 8:28).

10 Affirmations of Gratitude:
Start your day with an attitude of gratitude.

1. I am grateful for another day and another opportunity.

2. I am grateful for the blood and oxygen pumping through my body that is keeping me alive.

3. I am grateful for my ability to see, smell, taste, hear and feel.

4. I am grateful for God's grace and love for me.

5. I am grateful for the blessings that I have.

6. I am grateful for the abundance in my life.

7. I am grateful for my dreams and desires because I know that they are manifesting now.
8. I am so grateful for supportive friends and a loving family.
9. I am grateful for this moment.
10. I am grateful for learning and growing.

Create a Routine for Yourself:

What are your M.I.T.s (Most Important Things) during this season of your life?

6AM—Wake up and start your mental training (write in a journal, read for growth, meditate, listen to soft music, sip on some tea/coffee in silence) *no social media during this time

6:30AM—Workout (run, jog, walk, or lift weights)

7AM—Shower while listening to upbeat music, sing and dance around the house. Recite your positive affirmations out loud

8AM—Start homework/work

10AM—Movement break (walk, lunges, or air squats)

10:30AM—Read for pleasure or listen to a podcast

11:30AM—Connect with family and friends on social media

12PM—Lunch

12:30PM—Schoolwork/work

2:30PM—Call, text, or FaceTime a friend/loved one

*Use this template as an example to create your own routine/schedule.

Mental Training:

1. Wake up early and pray
2. Grab a hot cup of black coffee or tea in silence
3. Recite positive affirmations out loud
4. Complete a mindfulness or deep breathing exercise
5. Write down 3–5 things that I am grateful for in my journal
6. Read my Bible and meditate on the scriptures
7. Work out

*Use this template as an example to create your own program for mental training, or feel free to use this one.

REFERENCES & RESOURCES

[1] "The Number One Habit to Develop in Order to Feel More Positive." (2016.) Amen Clinics. Accessed August 9, 2020. https://www.amenclinics.com/blog/number-one-habit-develop-order-feel-positive/.

[2] "Suicide in America: Frequently Asked Questions." (n.d.) National Institute of Mental Health. Accessed August 9, 2020. https://www.nimh.nih.gov/health/publications/suicide-faq/index.shtml.

[3] Quinnett, Paul G. (2012.) *Suicide: The Forever Decision.*

[4] National Suicide Prevention Lifeline: https://suicidepreventionlifeline.org/.

[5] notOK App™ for download: www.notokapp.com.

[6] *Demi Lovato: Simply Complicated* official documentary link: https://www.youtube.com/watch?v=ZWTlL_w8cRA&t=1196s.

[7] Depression Test courtesy of Mental Health America: https://screening.mhanational.org/screening-tools/depression.

[8] Winfield, Chris. (2015.) "How to Stop Negative Thinking with 3 Simple Steps." Inc. Accessed August 9, 2020. https://www.inc.com/chris-winfield/is-stomping-ants-the-key-to-living-a-happier-life.html.

ABOUT THE AUTHOR

Abraham Sculley is a husband, educator, author, fitness trainer, and highly sought-after mental health speaker. He received his B.A. in Psychology from the University of West Florida in 2019 and currently lives in Pensacola, FL with his wife Estefania Sculley and dog Gypsy.

Abraham uses his personal story and professional expertise in the field of mental health to conduct suicide prevention training programs, host mental health awareness workshops, and educate others about the stigma of mental illness and the importance of prioritizing their mental health.

Over the last six years, Abraham has impacted numerous audiences around the United States, including professionals in health care organizations, leaders in for-profit organizations, nationally acclaimed non-profit agencies, and students and professors at major universities and colleges.

As the founder of Speaks 2 Inspire, LLC, an organization dedicated to promoting mental health awareness and sharing the mental health stories of others, Abraham continues to provide mental health education and follow his passion of assisting others in achieving optimal mental, emotional, and spiritual health.

Let's Connect!

Email: info@abrahamsculley.com

Website: www.abrahamsculley.com

Instagram: www.instagram.com/abrahamsculley

Facebook: www.facebook.com/abrahamsculleyspeaks

Twitter: www.twitter.com/speaks2inspire

YouTube: Abraham Speaks2Inspire

UNLEARN
THE
LIES